COSTING FOR THE
FASHION INDUSTRY

COSTING FOR THE FASHION INDUSTRY

Michael Jeffrey and Nathalie Evans

BERG

Oxford · New York

English edition
First published in 2011 by

Berg

Editorial offices:
First Floor, Angel Court, 81 St Clements Street, Oxford OX4 1AW, UK
175 Fifth Avenue, New York, NY 10010, USA

Berg is an imprint of Bloomsbury Publishing Plc.

Library of Congress Cataloging-in-Publication Data
A catalogue record for this book is available from the Library of Congress.

British Library Cataloguing-in-Publication Data
A catalogue record for this book is available from the British Library.

ISBN 978 1 84788 260 8 (Cloth)
  978 1 84788 259 2 (Paper)
  978 1 84788 735 1 (e-ind)

Typeset by Apex CoVantage, LLC, Madison, WI.

Printed in the UK by the MPG Books Group

www.bergpublishers.com

ACKNOWLEDGEMENT

The preparation of a textbook can be a lonely job and it is therefore useful to have the assistance of colleagues who offer help and advice. We are indebted to and would like to thank all those (too numerous to mention) in the Hollings Faculty at the Manchester Metropolitan University who have helped or supported us in the production of this work.

We would particularly like to thank for their help and encouragement with this work our colleagues Angela Peers for her encouragement of this work over a long period of time, Collin Lawton for testing out some of the exercise material, Gaynor Lea-Greenwood for proofreading some of the chapters and Professor Richard Murray for his broad support of the work.

CONTENTS

INTRODUCTION

Students are attracted to the fashion industry for a whole host of reasons—they like fashion, they are enthusiastic about clothes and fabrics, they see it as a vibrant global industry that they want to be involved in, they see it as an extension of the pop culture and they have a desire to be a part of this industry. This has been fuelled in recent years by glossy magazines, television programmes and shows like 'Clothes Show Live'. The recruitment to university and college fashion programmes over the last decade has steadily increased, and whilst only a small number of these graduates will end up as designers a high proportion will find employment in the industry in a range of jobs throughout the fashion supply chain.

Parents and advisors of students often think that because clothing manufacture in the UK has declined significantly that this is a twilight industry. Nothing could be further from the truth; the fashion industry is a vibrant multi-billion-dollar global industry with exciting international job opportunities. We all have more clothes in our wardrobes than ever before, and there are more and more specialist performance garments available than ever before. The interest in fashion and clothes also extends much later into life because the current older generation have been used to choice and style and are likely to continue that interest into their retirement. The future is very buoyant for the industry and the graduate jobs in the fashion supply chain are set to increase.

The challenges that the industry faces are also significant and will bring a new perspective to employment. Some of these challenges relate to the environment and its protection, others to ethical issues, others to rapidly changing technology, others to the shifting base of the fashion industry but all will provide new graduate entrants to the industry with a varied and potentially fascinating career.

Once students start their studies they often find the technical parts of the programme difficult—design is more exacting than they expected, pattern construction is quite mathematical and computers play an increasing part in the industry. They also find that fashion is a hard-nosed industry that has to make profits and part of that profit making is in the containment of costs. That might be the containment of manufacturing costs or the containment of sourcing costs, but either way it will impact on the final price point of the garment and the profit margins to be obtained.

This book is intended for those wanting an understanding of costing in relation to the clothing/fashion industry. The objective of the book is to introduce the reader to the principles of costing and the terminology used to give them an understanding of the composition of cost and a vocabulary of terms that will be useful when considering costing issues. It is intended to do this in a non-confrontational way and to introduce the numeracy gradually. We would stress that there are no complicated mathematical processes involved in the work; an ability to add, subtract, multiply and divide will be sufficient, though a pocket calculator will be useful in dealing with the numerical applications.

The book starts with a consideration of what is involved in garment manufacture. This is essentially the conversion of fabric and cloth into wearable garments, and it is important that design and buying students have a concept of these processes. That manufacture may not necessarily take place in the UK or even in Europe and the modern fashion industry may be sourcing garments from far-flung places around the world, but the manufacturing processes are broadly the same.

The costing aspect of the book starts with the elements of cost and product cost but also looks at other issues like marginal costing, standard costing, the changing nature of cost and new ideas relating to product cost such as activity-based costing. It also gives an introduction to capital investment appraisal as this is also an area where students may become involved once in employment in the industry. However, this is presented entirely within the context of the clothing/fashion industry with examples that reflect this.

The book also includes chapters that relate to the global nature of the fashion industry and the costs incurred when sourcing garments overseas, to reflect the current nature of the industry in the UK and Europe. Each chapter also has a small bibliography of additional reading and references that will enable students to read further about topics of interest or topics that are essential to their programme. A more detailed bibliography is given at the end of the work.

It is intended that this book will be of use to clothing and fashion students who will find it easier to relate to than the standard textbooks on cost accounting. The book does not contain the detailed technical issues that might be found in a standard cost accounting text; if more detail in these areas is required, then the student should refer to standard accounting texts, some of which are detailed at the end of the chapters. This book may also be of use to those already employed in the fashion industry to give them a better understanding of the principles of costing applied to their industry and provide a formal structure for what they have learned in practice.

The book is not specifically written for students of accountancy, though those involved in the apparel industry may find it useful to help put their generic studies into a specific industry context.

The book contains some information on recording costs but does not go into the detail of cost accounts and their reconciliation with the financial accounts of the business. Nor, on a technical point, does it deal with the issue of over/underabsorption where absorption costing systems are in use. Similarly the book does not concern itself with detailed computer applications; it is essentially about the principles. The book does not concern itself with financial accounting or taxation issues. These are different subjects and would require different texts and a different focus.

The chapters in the book contain activities and exercises to enable the student to understand the content of each chapter and to practise the methods shown. Doing these activities and exercises will assist the learning process. Model answers to most of the exercises are given at the end of the book, but do not look at these until you have attempted the exercise yourself.

In addition to the reading detailed at the end of chapters in the book, we also suggest that reading journals and magazines is a good way to be up to date with the latest developments in the industry. The following periodicals will help with the global context of your broader studies of the fashion industry and also give you a concept of the extent of jobs available in the industry.

The Journal of Fashion Marketing and Management
DR—Drapers Record
Menswear
Textile Horizons
Textile International

Also, for a broader understanding of the global fashion industry we would recommend the book *The Apparel Industry* (2nd edn) by our colleague Richard Jones as a definitive work on the industry and a book all fashion students should read.

We wish you well with your studies and hope that this book provides a light onto what might otherwise seem a daunting topic.

1

THE NATURE OF CLOTHING MANUFACTURE
AND THE NEED FOR COSTING

Introduction

This chapter seeks to explain the nature of clothing manufacture and the need for costing in the industry. It introduces the student to the basic processes and some basic terminology used in clothing manufacture.

What Is Clothing Manufacture?

At the outset we should perhaps take a little time to consider exactly what we mean by *clothing manufacture* and the processes involved. This may be important for those readers who have not worked in a clothing factory or even had the opportunity to visit a clothing manufacturer. If you are not familiar with the processes involved in clothing manufacture, then a visit to a factory would be advisable as this would put into perspective the issues considered in this book.

In very simple terms *clothing manufacture* is the conversion of fabrics (cloth) into wearable garments. To effect this conversion the fabrics have to be cut into component parts, which are passed through a series of processes to produce the garment. Broadly speaking these are the processes in clothing manufacture.

- The pattern pieces are planned to form a marker—this indicates how the component parts of the garment will be cut out of the fabric.
- The fabric is spread often several plies high to form a lay.
- The pattern pieces that form the component pieces of the garment are cut out of the fabric.
- Some of the component pieces are fused with a fusible interlining to give reinforcement.
- The pieces then pass through a series of sewing operations; during these operations other materials may be introduced, e.g. zips, buttons, or lace.

- The completed garment is pressed, has loose threads removed and is inspected for quality.
- The finished garment is then packed.

Whilst this is to some extent an oversimplification of the processes involved, it at least gives an idea of what the average factory will be involved in. From this the reader can see that the factory will have to provide three things:

- materials—fabric, thread, etc.
- labour—workers to perform the various manufacturing tasks
- an environment, equipped with the right machinery, to enable the processing to be done

Not all factories will be involved in all the processes; for example a factory making just denim jeans will not have a fusing operation as this garment does not have any fused parts. However, a jeans factory might have a stonewashing operation to give the jeans a fashionable look, or alternatively the stonewashing might be done by an outside contractor.

Similarly, not all the processes need to be done in the same factory, and very large manufacturers sometimes rationalize their operations by cutting the fabrics in one factory, and that cutting operation supplies several other factories with cut parts to make into garments. This may particularly be the case where a manufacturer has invested in high-tech equipment at a high capital cost and needs to maximize the use of such equipment.

Students wanting a more detailed picture of clothing manufacture are referred to one of the standard textbooks on clothing production. A reading list appears at the end of this chapter.

Two Important Questions

For a book dealing with costing in relation to the clothing industry the following two questions are important:

- What is cost?
- Why do we need to cost our garments?

Before reading on in this chapter, think about these two issues, and perhaps jot down how you would explain the meaning of 'cost' and why you think a manufacturer should be concerned with cost and the process of costing.

Definition of Cost

Cost is the economic value placed upon the resources consumed to make a product.

By economic value we mean a monetary value expressed in terms of the appropriate units of currency. That might be pounds sterling (£) in the UK, dollars ($) in the USA and other parts of the world or the Euro (€) more widely in Europe.

To make a product (and remember that clothes or garments are products), the manufacturer will have to use resources—materials, labour and a variety of services and other capital resources such as the use of premises. The quantity of these resources used, expressed as a monetary value, is the cost of the product.

Cost might be expressed as relating to individual products, i.e. individual garments (unit cost), a number of products (batch cost) or a specific order from a customer producing perhaps several thousand garments (job cost).

Alternatively, cost can be expressed relating to time—the costs incurred for a month, a quarter or a half year or a full year.

The Need for Costing

Cost also has a relationship to the price of the product, the price being what the manufacturer's customer or client will pay for the garments produced. Clearly, to make a profit the manufacturer will need the price to be more than the cost. Thus, when determining the price or negotiating the price of a garment the manufacturer will need to have a good understanding of the costs to ensure that the price covers the costs.

The following are the main reasons why a clothing manufacturer needs to be involved in costing and have an understanding of the costs. It is useful if designers, pattern cutters and garment technologists also have an understanding of the costs.

Pricing decisions. If the manufacturer produces a branded product or sells directly to the end user of the garment, i.e. direct to the public, then it may determine the selling price of the garment. The most commonly used method of pricing is *full-cost pricing*, where a percentage profit or markup is added to the cost of the product. The percentage profit, or markup, may be determined based on an agreed company policy taking into account what the market will bear in terms of price for that product.

Thus, to make pricing decisions the manufacturer needs to know the cost of the product.

Acceptance decisions. This is probably more common in clothing manufacture and occurs when a retailer instructs a manufacturer to make a particular garment but is prepared to pay only a stated price. Here the retailer is in the driving seat in terms of fixing the price that will be paid; thus, to decide whether to accept this work the manufacturer needs to know what it will cost him to make that garment. This is an acceptance decision—do I take this work at this price and if I do will I make any profit, or, knowing what my costs are, do I try to renegotiate the price?

Thus to make the acceptance decision the manufacturer needs to know the cost of the product.

Tendering. Though this is less common in the clothing industry than in the building industry, it is a situation that may arise. Here the customer advertises in the trade press for a manufacturer to make a specific garment or job of garments. The work will have to be carried out to a detailed specification and manufacturers will be invited to submit a 'tender', i.e. a price for doing the job. The customer, subject to checking that the manufacturer can do the job, will usually select the lowest tender.

Thus to make a viable tender the manufacturer needs to know his costs.

Cost control. It is also important for manufacturers to keep control of their costs. The profit margins in clothing manufacture tend to be rather slim; thus ensuring that excessive cost does not erode those margins is important. The manufacturer who does not measure his costs cannot hope to control them. Therefore, measuring, recording and comparing costs are all part of the control process to ensure the ongoing profitability of the business.

Profit. People are in business essentially to make a profit. There may be other laudable reasons for being in business—making use of one's talents, providing employment for the family, and so forth—and small craft businesses may not always place the profit motive at the top of their list of priorities. However, the profit motive is important if the business is to provide a living for those running it and those employed by it.

The profit of a business is measured over periods of time, usually a year, in the financial accounts of the business. There is, however, a link between the costing and the financial accounts in that if the product costing is done badly and jobs are accepted at or under cost, then at the end of the year the business will not make any profit. It may be expedient for a manufacturer to accept some work at cost or even under cost, but generally this should be the exception.

This book does not deal with the financial accounts of the business. Students wanting a more detailed understanding of this aspect of accounting should consult one of the standard accounting texts; see the reading list at the end of this chapter.

From Manufacture to Sourcing

At one time clothing manufacture was widespread in the UK with many types of garments being produced for both the domestic and overseas markets. This was also the case throughout much of Europe, but this is no longer the situation as rising labour costs in the UK and Western Europe have tended to force retailers to seek garments produced by low-cost manufacturers overseas. The retail houses are much less concerned with the manufacturing costs and are more concerned with the costs of sourcing garments from suppliers. Nowadays, apart from some specialist suppliers and some suppliers who may be prepared to produce short runs of garments, it is likely that those suppliers will be based overseas. This introduces new elements into the costs relating to sourcing the garments—including issues like freight, warehousing, insurance and so forth.

These developments in the industry and this aspect of costing will be dealt with in more detail in Chapters 5 and 6.

Exercises and Activities

1. If you have not been in a clothing factory, it would be useful to arrange a visit to a clothing manufacturer. If you are following a course of study, visiting several factories of different types over the duration of your course would be useful. This is particularly important for fashion students, as well as technology students, as it will give you an understanding of how a manufacturer will put your designs into production.
2. Read the earlier chapters of one of the clothing production textbooks (see references at the end of this chapter) to assist with your understanding of clothing manufacture.
3. Have a really good look through your own wardrobe. Look at how garments are constructed and the different materials used in their construction. If possible look at the origin of the garments to see which countries they have been sourced from.
4. Think about clothing manufacture and then list under three headings—*materials, labour and other*—the resources required to make garments. Use Table 1.1 if you like. Remember that costing is essentially about placing a value on the use of these resources.

TABLE 1.1

Materials	Labour	Other

Further Reading

Production
Brown, P. (2001), *Ready Wear Apparel Analysis* (3rd edn), Harlow: Prentice Hall.
Carr, H., and Latham, B. (2008), *Carr and Latham's Technology of Clothing Manufacture* (4th edn), revised by Tyler, D., Oxford: Blackwell.
Chuter, A. J. (1995), *Introduction to Clothing Production Management* (2nd edn), Oxford: Blackwell Science.
Cooklin, G. (1997), *Garment Technology for Fashion Designers*, Oxford: Blackwell Science.
Cooklin, G. (2006), *Introduction to Clothing Manufacture*, revised by Hayes, S. G., and McLoughlin, J., Oxford: Blackwell Science.
Fairhurst, C., ed. (2008), *Advances in Apparel Production*, Cambridge: Woodhead.

Financial Accounting
Ryan, B. (2004), *Finance and Accounting for Business*, London: Thomson.
Wood, F., and Sangster, A. (2008), *Frank Wood's Business Accounting 1* (11th edn), New York: Financial Times/Prentice Hall.

Broader Fashion Industry
Jones, R. M. (2006), *The Apparel Industry* (2nd edn), Oxford: Blackwell.

2

THE ELEMENTS OF COST

Introduction

This chapter seeks to explain the *elements of cost* as a means of classifying cost in a way that can be used in cost accounting. At the end of the chapter the student should be able to identify the main elements of cost and relate those to a clothing manufacturing situation.

Classification of Cost

There are a number of ways in which costs can be classified. In this book we use three methods of classification:

- The detailed breakdown of cost into its elements—*the elements of cost*
- The behaviour of cost—*fixed and variable costs* (see Chapters 7 and 8)
- The activities that generate cost—*activity-based costing* (see Chapter 11)

This chapter is concerned with the elements of costs. This classification is used extensively in recording costs over periods of time and is used in traditional methods of product costing. The detailed elements of cost give a good understanding of the costs within our manufacturing business, and you should become familiar with them. The terminology used in the elements of cost will also give you a good vocabulary of terms used in manufacture and costing.

Cost can be summarized into three main categories (see Figure 2.1):

Direct materials—the materials that become the garment
Direct labour—the wages cost of the operators who make the garments
Overheads—all the other costs of running the business

Figure 2.1 also shows the approximate split of these costs in garment manufacture.

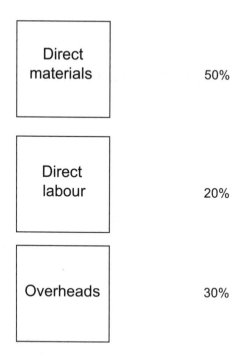

Figure 2.1 The three main categories of cost.

Note from this diagram that the direct materials cost forms about half the cost of the finished garment. Thus the control and costing of the direct materials are vital in that they represent such a large element of the cost.

These three main elements can be analyzed into a more detailed picture, known as the *elements of cost*, illustrated in Figure 2.2. You should study this diagram with the text and become familiar with the elements of cost.

Direct Costs

Direct Materials Cost

Essentially the direct materials cost is the cost of the materials that form the finished garments. In clothing manufacture it is the largest element of cost, representing between 45 and 60 per cent of the garment cost. Thus on average it is about half the total cost.

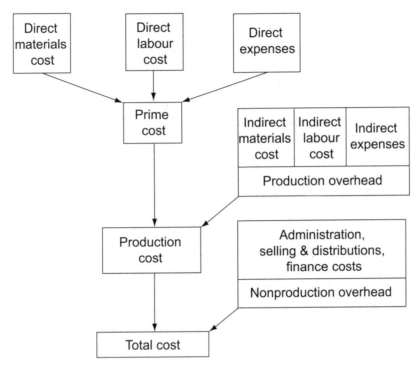

Figure 2.2 The elements of cost.

Whilst the following is not a comprehensive list, it gives a good guide to the extent of the direct materials:

fabric (cloth), linings, thread, interlinings, buttons, zips, trimmings, shoulder pads, sleeve head roll, batting (fibre filling), elastic, studs, hook-and-eye fasteners, lace, press-studs, Velcro, seam binding, labels

All materials that form part of the garment need to be accounted for in the cost, and this is usually done *at cost*, i.e. the price paid for the material. It normally includes any carriage costs incurred in transporting the materials from the supplier to the manufacturer, this is sometimes referred to as *carriage inwards*.

Take a close look at the garments in your wardrobe and note the different materials that make up the garment. Clearly the main fabric of the garment will be the biggest part of the cost, but all the other materials also need to be accounted for. In shirt manufacture the small white pearl buttons may cost only fractions of a penny each, but with eight buttons on each shirt and tens of thousands of shirts being produced, this becomes a significant figure.

The cost of the fabric and lining will be the largest component of the direct materials cost. If savings are to be made it will usually be in this area. The initial costing of fabrics and linings is based on *lay plans,* or plans of how the pattern pieces will be spread on the fabric. Once the fabric goes into production, however, this initial costing will be improved upon because the production lay planners and cutters usually get better utilization of the fabric than can be done at the design stage.

The *utilization of the fabric* is the degree of economy achieved in cutting the pattern pieces out of the fabric. This needs to be done with minimal wastage and is usually expressed as a percentage. A high percentage indicates good utilization of the fabric.

The fabric is usually cut several plies high, and the lay planner takes great care in drawing the configuration of pattern pieces that will be placed upon the plies of fabric. The drawing of the pattern pieces is known as the *marker plan*. The planner may try a number of placements seeking to get the best positioning of the pattern pieces and thus the best utilization of the fabric. Computer-based lay planning systems are available, with a view to assisting the planner in maximizing the efficiency of the marker plan.

See the reading list at the end of this chapter for more information about the lay planning and cutting of fabrics.

Most garments are sewn together with thread. Whilst the consumption of thread in the construction of a garment is not a major part of the direct materials cost of the individual garment, it may represent a significant amount of the cost when large quantities of garments are being made. Garments that have seams constructed using three-, four- and five-thread machines will require significantly more thread than garments sewn together on a lock-stitch machine, and thus the cost of such garments will be higher. Garments that have smocking on them will also require large quantities of thread, and this will increase their cost.

Factories often estimate the thread cost. Care should be taken, however, to ensure that the cost is not underestimated or significantly overestimated.

The major sewing thread manufacturers publish guidance on thread consumption; see the reading list at the end of this chapter. Gutermann, the German thread manufacturer, have also developed a computer programme to enable manufacturers to calculate with some accuracy the extent of thread consumption. However, a manufacturer must consider whether expenditure on such software is cost-effective for what in many cases is a small amount of the cost.

The figures quoted by the manufacturers are only a guide and may be adversely affected by the density of the fabrics used. However, here is an example of thread consumption for two plies of fabric sewn at seven stitches per centimetre:

Lock-stitch machine: 2.5 cm of thread per cm of seam
5-thread safety stitch machine: 20 cm of thread per cm of seam

Based on such figures, a standard ladies' blouse might require upward of 70 metres of thread.

Interlinings

Interlinings are used as reinforcement in parts of garments such as collars, cuffs, waistbands, and the fronts of jackets. They may be sewn in or attached by fusing to the garment using a fusing press. Interlinings are available in a wide variety of weights and types. Although per garment they may be used in relatively small quantities, the amount may be significant when producing a run of garments. In respect of stock control, fusible interlinings have a limited shelf life, and therefore arrangements for their purchase and control are important.

Again, care needs to be taken in costing out the interlinings, and this should not be underestimated.

Fastenings

Most garments will have some form of fastening. Fastenings might include buttons, zips, press studs, hook and loop fasteners, or Velcro.

Individually these may represent a small amount of cost, but in quantity they form a significant cost and need inclusion. Special buttons and fastenings purchased for a specific job, such as horn buttons or large zips, may be relatively expensive and therefore need careful costing.

Other Direct Materials

All other direct materials costs need to be included in the costing, and care needs to be taken to ensure that all materials used in the construction of the garment are accounted for. This may include the cost of maker or brand labels, garment care labels and in some cases the cost of the packaging materials. Where the garment is sold as a packed product—e.g. a boxed men's shirt—the packaging cost forms part of the direct materials cost of the product.

In conclusion, remember that approximately half the cost of the garment is in the direct materials. Thus this is the most important element of the cost.

Direct Labour Cost

Labour cost is essentially the wages of people who work in the business. By *direct labour* we mean the wages cost of those people who are engaged in making the garments. Thus it is the wages cost of lay planners and cutters, fusing press operators, sewing machine operators, press room staff and in some cases those involved in packing the garment.

The lay planning and cutting staff may take several hours to do their part of the manufacturing process. The production manager will probably have a good idea of how many staff will need to be involved and how much time will be required for specific jobs. Thus the labour hours required multiplied by the hourly wage rate will give the amount of direct labour cost. Remember that if three people are involved in the cutting, and a job takes them three hours, then that represents nine direct labour hours (3 hours × 3 people). The lay planners and cutters will usually be the most highly paid direct labour operatives, as this has traditionally been seen as a very skilled job.

The fusing and sewing operations are also based on the time required to perform the operation. Because some of these tasks can be performed very quickly, the time values attached to them will be expressed in minutes or fractions of a minute. These time values are known as *standard minute values*, or *SMVs*. These SMVs can be achieved through the use of work-study techniques in which a trained work-study assessor takes timings of the operation. Alternatively, the timings of the sewing operations can be assessed by use of one of the commercially available database systems, *General Sewing Data* (GSD) or some similar system.

The extent of the standard minutes required for a job are converted into hours, often referred to as *standard hours*, and then multiplied by the appropriate hourly rate to achieve the direct labour cost. The hourly rates will vary for different operators, for example a fusing press operator will be paid less than a trained sewing machine operator, and experienced machinists will usually be paid more than newly trained operators. Thus a range of direct labour wage rates may have to be used to achieve the total direct labour cost.

Most factories, other than the very smallest ones, will be organized into departments often called *cost centres* (more will be said about this in Chapter 4). In the factory these departments will be based around the manufacturing processes that need to be performed. In clothing these will be, broadly, laying up and cutting, fusing, sewing, pressing and packing. Thus the direct labour cost for a job passing through the factory will be calculated department by department depending on the direct labour processes required for that job.

In the UK we would usually expect the direct labour cost to represent about 20 per cent of the total cost. However, as greater mechanization is introduced into the industry this percentage may be eroded. Many garment retailers in recent years have sought to reduce the production costs of their garments, and this has often meant seeking production overseas, usually to areas of lower direct labour cost, with a view to containing this element of cost.

Direct Expenses

Direct expenses constitute the last of the direct costs and are the least significant in terms of percentage of cost. A direct expense is a cost without which that specific garment cannot be manufactured. Examples of direct expenses include the following:

The cost of stonewashing denim garments to achieve a fashionable look where this work is contracted out to an external factory.

The cost of putting embroidery on to a garment where it is contracted out to an external factory

The cost of a licence to produce a garment that has a copyrighted figure or motif on it, e.g. a sweatshirt with the Bart Simpson cartoon character on it

The royalty payable to a designer for the use of her design work—though this is not very common in the fashion industry

Prime Cost

The *prime cost* is the basic cost of producing the garment and is the sum total of the direct costs. Thus:

direct materials + direct labour + direct expenses = prime cost

Indirect Costs—The Overheads

Clearly in running a factory there are many other costs beyond the direct costs of producing the garments. These are often referred to as the *indirect costs*, or, more commonly, the *overheads*. In the USA these costs are called *the burden*.

The overheads are all the other costs of running the factory and the business. These represent about 30 per cent of the total cost, though in some cases they may be more. The changing nature of these costs is considered in a later chapter.

The overheads are usually split into two groups (see Figure 2.2)—those concerned with manufacture and that can be identified with the factory, known as *production overheads*, and those that relate to the administration, marketing and finance of the business, known as *non-production overheads*. In small manufacturing units the nonproduction overheads will be relatively small; however, large manufacturers often find that their nonproduction overheads become significantly large as the management and administration of the business increase.

Production Overheads

Production overheads are the indirect costs of running the factory or production unit. From Figure 2.2 it can be seen that they involve indirect materials, indirect labour and indirect expenses.

Indirect Materials Cost

Indirect materials are any materials consumed in the factory that do not form part of the completed garment. They might include small replacement component parts for machinery (needles, belts etc.), lubricants, coolants, cleaning materials, food for the staff canteen and so forth.

Indirect Labour Cost

As already mentioned, labour costs are the wages costs of employing staff. Indirect labour is the wages cost of people who are employed in the factory but do not actually work producing garments. These might include caretaking (janitorial) staff, maintenance workers, cleaners, work-study officers, supervisory management, storeroom staff, the factory personnel officer and factory management.

Indirect Expenses Cost

Indirect expenses are the other costs of providing the factory, its equipment and its running costs. They might include rental of the factory unit, the business rates on the factory,[1] insurance, services to provide heat, light and power (i.e. gas, water, electricity), telephone and the capital costs of the machinery and equipment.

Production Cost

The *production cost* comprises the *prime cost* plus the *production overhead* (see Figure 2.2). Thus:

prime cost + production overhead = production cost

Non-production Overheads

From Figure 2.2 it can be seen that the nonproduction overheads broadly include the selling, distribution, administration and finance costs of the business.

Selling and Distribution Costs

Selling and distribution costs might include sales staff wages and salaries, warehousing costs, rental of a showroom, the large-scale packing of the product, freight and haulage costs, sales promotion and advertising costs and exhibition costs.

Administration Costs

Administration costs might include office staff salaries, rental of the offices, business rates of the offices, stationery, accountancy fees, office machinery costs as well as heat, light and power costs of the office.

Finance Costs

Finance cost might include bank charges, loan interest, overdraft interest and costs involved in arranging loans.

In conclusion, the *total cost* is the *production cost* plus the *nonproduction overhead* (see Figure 2.2). Thus:

production cost + nonproduction overheads = total cost

Summary of the Elements of Cost

direct materials + direct labour + direct expenses

=

prime cost

+

production overhead

=

production cost

+

nonproduction overhead

=

TOTAL COST

Exercises and Activities

1. Using Exercise Table 2.1, analyse the following direct costs and place each one under its respective elements of cost. The first one has been done as an example.
    (a) cutters' wages
    (b) woollen worsted cloth
    (c) lock-stitch machinists' wages
    (d) thread
    (e) licence to use a copyright motif
    (f) interlining
    (g) melton for collars
    (h) press room staff wages
    (i) specially sourced bone buttons
    (j) stonewashing done externally
    (k) fusing press operators' wages
    (l) royalty to a designer
    (m) sleeve lining
    (n) linen cloth
    (o) lace trimming
    (p) buttonholers' wages

EXERCISE TABLE 2.1

Direct Materials	Direct Labour	Direct Expenses
	a	

(q) fabric finishing treatment done externally
(r) hire of a specialist machine required for a specific job
(s) packing material for a packed shirt

2. Using Exercise Table 2.2, analyse the following costs and place each one into its appropriate classification. The first one has been done as an example.
   (a) fabric for dresses
   (b) sewing machinists' wages
   (c) interlinings
   (d) rental of factory unit
   (e) cutters' wages
   (f) fusing press operators' wages
   (g) factory manager's salary
   (h) factory maintenance staff wages
   (i) administration staff salaries
   (j) packing costs
   (k) loan interest
   (l) buttons for a blouse
   (m) delivery van drivers' wages
   (n) thread used in production
   (o) staff canteen costs
   (p) pressing staff wages
   (q) maintenance of office machinery
   (r) royalty for a 'Snoopy' motif used on a T-shirt
   (s) cleaning staff wages
   (t) work-study staff wages
   (u) stonewashing done externally
   (v) business rates on factory
   (w) rental of office premises

(x) zips used in production
(y) buttonholers' wages
(z) bank charges

EXERCISE TABLE 2.2

Direct Materials	Direct Labour	Direct Expenses	Production Overhead	Non-Production Overhead
a				

EXERCISE TABLE 2.3

Indirect Materials	Indirect Labour	Indirect Expenses
a		

3. Using Exercise Table 2.3, classify the following production overheads into their respective indirect elements of cost. The first one has been done as an example.
   (a) sewing machine needles
   (b) factory manager's salary
   (c) work-study officer's wages
   (d) cleaning staff wages
   (e) rental of the factory unit
   (f) lubricants for machinery
   (g) business rates on the factory

(h) factory insurance
(i) supervisors' wages
(j) factory power, heat and light
(k) cleaning materials
(l) factory personnel officer's wages
(m) maintenance staff wages
(n) designer/pattern cutters' wages
(o) pattern paper
(p) parts required to repair vacuum press

4. Using Exercise Table 2.4, classify the following nonproduction overheads into their respective indirect elements of cost. The first one has been done as an example.
(a) salesmen's salaries
(b) warehouse costs
(c) administration staff salaries
(d) receptionists' wages
(e) bank charges
(f) audit fees
(g) rent of the offices
(h) debenture interest
(i) delivery van drivers' wages
(j) maintenance of office machinery
(k) exhibition costs
(l) rental of showroom
(m) office manager's salary
(n) mortgage interest
(o) stationery costs
(p) photocopying

EXERCISE TABLE 2.4

Selling and Distribution Costs	Administration Costs	Finance Expenses
a	145	

Note

1. Business rates are a tax on business premises in the UK, collected by the local authority and intended as a contribution toward local services, e.g. refuse collection or street cleaning.

Further Reading

Carr, H., and Latham, B. (2008), *Carr and Latham's Technology of Clothing Manufacture* (4th edn), revised by Tyler, D., Oxford: Blackwell.

Cooklin, G. (2006), *Introduction to Clothing Manufacture*, revised by Hayes, S. G., and McLoughlin, J., Oxford: Blackwell Science.

J. & P. Coats Limited (1996), *The Technology of Seams and Threads*, Glasgow: Coats Ltd.

Russell, D., Patel, A., and Wilkinson-Riddle, G. (2002), *Cost Accounting: An Essential Guide*, Harlow, Prentice Hall.

Tyler, D. (1991), *Materials Management in Clothing Production*, Oxford: Blackwell Science.

3

COSTING OVER PERIODS OF TIME

Introduction

This chapter seeks to explain costing over periods of time—monthly, quarterly, half-yearly and so forth. It shows the development of costs over periods of time based on the elements of cost, and these are referred to in the chapter as period cost reports. The chapter deals with the treatment of stocks of direct materials, work-in-progress, accruals and prepayments and depreciation.

Period Cost Reports

A *period cost report* is where the costs of the business are reported over time. They are usually analysed based on the elements of cost and are reported monthly. These monthly reports are also often summarized quarterly, half-yearly and annually. The report enables the business to see, at a glance, its costs for the respective period and compare those costs with budgeted figures and with similar periods of time.

Some period cost reports might show the difference between the actual costs recorded for the period and the budgeted costs set for the period. These differences are often referred to as *variances*.

The Uses of Period Cost Reports

Control. As mentioned in Chapter 1 the profit margins in clothing manufacture are often slim; thus if costs are not controlled they may easily erode the profits. This regular reporting of the costs enables management to keep a close watch on them and their possible escalation. This is important for all costs incurred but particularly the overheads costs, which are often more difficult to control. By examining the period cost reports the manufacturer will be able to see that costs are falling within budgeted levels, i.e. planned levels. If costs are going over budget, then the period cost report gives early warning and action can be taken.

Thus cost control is an important feature of the period cost reports.

Comparison. Still on the theme of control, the period cost report enables management to compare costs with other months or other periods. This too is part of the control process and the process of making management cost-conscious.

Profit. Costs analysed in this way relate closely to the profitability of the business. The total cost for the period when compared with the sales revenue for the same period gives the net profit. The measurement of profit over periods of time is outside the scope of this book. Interested students should consult one of the standard financial accounting textbooks; see the Further Reading list at the end of Chapter 1.

Process Costing. A clothing manufacturer that makes the same type of garment again and again, as in the case of a jeans factory or a shirt factory, may adopt a form of unit costing known as process costing.

Unit costing is where you find the cost of making just one of a product—thus in process costing the manufacturer is trying to establish the cost of one garment.

In this system of costing the manufacturer calculates an *average unit cost*, i.e. an average cost per garment produced. This is done by taking the total cost for the period and dividing it by the number of garments produced in that period—resulting in the average cost per garment produced.

$$\frac{\text{total cost for the period}}{\text{garments produced}} = \text{average cost per garment}$$

This is known as process costing and is dealt with in more detail in Chapter 4.

Capital Equipment Costs

The costs in the period cost report are supposed to reflect as far as possible the costs for that period. However, businesses will inevitably purchase some items that are intended to be used for very long periods of time—in particular the purchase of equipment, furniture, machinery and the like—and this is known as *capital expenditure*. Examples of capital expenditure in a clothing factory might be pattern tables, cutting equipment, sewing equipment, and pressing equipment. Generally speaking, capital expenditures have a useful life exceeding one year.

Often the purchase of such equipment involves large sums of money. Clearly if all that capital cost is put into the period cost report for one month, then the total cost figure in that month will be highly inflated. Months with capital cost when compared to months that do not include any capital cost will be wildly different.

Thus the cost of such equipment is not included as such in the cost report. Instead the cost of capital equipment is spread out so that each month of its useful life bears a little of its cost. This share of the capital cost is known as the *depreciation*.

Whilst inevitably the calculation of the depreciation involves some estimation and therefore a degree of inaccuracy, at least the manufacturer makes a consistent attempt to spread the capital cost over the useful life of the equipment. The depreciation is treated as part of the overhead cost, and if it relates to the factory and production it will be part of the production overhead. If, however, the depreciation relates to the administration, selling and distribution aspect of the business, then it will be part of the non-production overhead.

There are a number of ways in which the capital equipment costs can be spread over their useful lives, but a common method is the straight-line method or equal instalment method.

Depreciation: The Straight-Line Method

In the straight-line method of depreciation the annual amount of depreciation of the capital equipment is calculated as follows:

$$\frac{\text{cost of the equipment} - \text{estimated scrap value}}{\text{estimated life}}$$

Having obtained an annual amount for depreciation in this way, we can divide the figure by 12 to give an amount per month.

Example

A clothing manufacturer purchases some new sewing equipment at a cost of £12,000. The equipment has an estimated life of 8 years and an estimated scrap value of £480.

$$\frac{£12,000 - £480}{8} = \frac{£11,520}{8}$$
$$= £1,440 \text{ depreciation cost per annum}$$
$$\frac{£1,440}{12} = £120 \text{ depreciation cost per month}$$

The period cost report each month would include £120 for the depreciation of this equipment, over the equipment's life.

The period cost report follows the elements of cost described in detail in Chapter 2, taking into account the adjustments described in this chapter. Thus it analyses the costs in the following way (Table 3.1):

TABLE 3.1

	£
Direct materials cost	
Direct labour cost	
Direct expenses	
Prime cost	
Production overhead	
Production cost	
Non-production overhead	
Total cost	

The amount of detail and the layout of the report will depend on the management of the business and how much detail and clarity they require. The following illustrations are typical of how the report might be constructed.

Period Cost Report: A Simple Illustration

The following cost information was extracted from the records of Arkan Fashions for the month of October (see Table 3.2).

This information can now be analysed over the elements of cost to produce a simple period cost report (see Table 3.3).

If you examine the report in Table 3.3, you will see that it takes the cost data for Arkan Fashions and analyses it over the elements of cost. Note that in the business rates entry (*), this cost has been split between the production overheads and the nonproduction overheads. You will often find costs like this in business where some of the cost relates to the factory and some to the non-production functions. Management has to decide how these costs will be split in order to give a suitable analysis of the costs.

This statement has analysed the costs using three columns, but it could involve more or fewer columns depending on the extent of the data and the degree of analysis that the management of the business require. In Table 3.3 you can see that the main elements of cost—direct material, direct labour, prime cost, and so forth—are totalled in the right-hand column, enabling management to see these costs easily. The composition of these costs is shown in the inner columns.

If you turn to the end of this chapter, Exercise Table 3.1 is a similar data set. Practice producing a simple period cost report before reading on.

TABLE 3.2

	£
Fabric	30,200
Buttons, trimmings etc.	1,580
Thread	1,650
Wages and salaries:	
Cutters	2,400
Machinists	6,400
Pressers	3,000
Supervisors	3,200
Factory management salaries	3,600
Administration staff salaries	2,600
Factory rent	8,000
Office rent	1,000
Business rates (75% factory, 25% office)	2,400
Sundry factory expenses	680
Bank charges and interest	250
Depreciation:	
Factory machinery	150
Factory furniture	100
Office furniture	50

Stocks and Inventory

The illustration of Arkan Fashions is useful for us to see the basic analysis of the period cost report, but in practice the issue of the direct materials cost is more complex. Most manufacturers will maintain some stocks of materials for use in production at a later stage. Direct materials bought in one month may not always go into production in that month but may be stored until they are required at a later date.

Some materials may be bought specifically for certain jobs in the factory, but other common materials may be kept in stock at all times, ready for use when required. In our period cost report we will endeavour to show the cost of the materials used in production—i.e. *cost of direct materials consumed*—and not the cost of the direct materials purchased in that period.

TABLE 3.3 Arkan Fashions period cost report—October

	£	£	£
Fabric		30,200	
Buttons, trimmings		1,580	
Thread		1,650	
Direct materials cost			33,430
Cutters' wages		2,400	
Machinists' wages		6,400	
Pressers' wages		3,000	
Direct labour cost			11,800
Prime cost			**45,230**
Supervisors' wages	3,200		
Factory management salaries	3,600		
Indirect labour cost		6,800	
Factory rent		8,000	
Business rates		1,800*	
Sundry expenses		680	
Depreciation:			
Machinery	150		
Furniture	100	250	
Production overheads			17,530
Production cost			**62,760**
Admin. salaries		2,600	
Office rent		1,000	
Business rates		600*	
Bank charges		250	
Depreciation:			
Office furniture		50	
Non-production overheads			4,500
Total cost			**67,260**

To do this, the period cost report has to take account of the cost of the direct materials held in stock at both the beginning and the end of the period. The stocks of materials held at the beginning of the period are known as *opening stock*, and the stocks left at the end of the period are known as *closing stock*. The cost of the direct materials consumed in the period is calculated as follows:

value of the opening stock of direct materials

+

cost of direct materials purchased in the period

−

value of the closing stock of direct materials

=

cost of direct materials consumed

Example

A jeans manufacturer uses large quantities of blue denim fabric and makes regular purchases of this fabric, maintaining stocks ready to go into production.

At the beginning of January the manufacturer was holding 13,000 metres of blue denim which had cost £18,200. During the month of January a further 39,000 metres were purchased at a cost of £52,650. At the end of January the factory was holding in stock 19,000 metres of the fabric, which had cost £25,650.

The cost of the blue denim fabric consumed in the January period is:

	£
opening stock of direct materials	18,200
Add purchases of direct materials	52,650
	70,850
Less closing stock of direct materials	25,650
cost of direct materials consumed	45,200

The value of the stocks of materials or inventory is generally calculated based on the cost of those materials, i.e. what the manufacturer paid or will have to pay for them. If the manufacturer has to pay a delivery cost on materials, this is usually included in the cost of those materials. Such a cost is often referred to as *carriage inwards*.

In the preceding illustration only one direct material, blue denim, was considered, but clearly in a clothing factory many fabrics and materials are used. Table 3.4 illustrates how the direct materials cost might be handled when a number of materials are involved.

Table 3.4 simplifies the situation where a range of direct materials are used. The values of the opening stocks of direct materials at the beginning of the month are shown in column 1. The purchases of the direct materials in the month are shown in column 2. Column 3 is the opening stock plus the purchases of direct materials. Column 4 shows the value of the closing stock and column 5 the direct materials consumed. At the bottom of the table the

TABLE 3.4

Material	1	2	3	4	5
	£	£	£	£	£
Blue denim	1,200	8,400	9,600	1,650	7,950
Grey denim	800	6,700	7,500	1,500	6,000
Stone corduroy	4,300	0	4,300	1,200	3,100
Green corduroy	850	5,700	6,550	2,100	4,450
Grey poly cotton	750	4,400	5,150	800	4,350
Calico	230	3,500	3,730	350	3,380
Totals for month	8,130	28,700	36,830	7,600	29,230

TABLE 3.5

	£
Opening stock of direct materials	8,130
Add purchases of direct materials	28,700
	36,830
Less closing stock of direct materials	7,600
Cost of direct materials used	29,230

totals for the month are shown, and these are the figures that would appear in the period cost report, as depicted in Table 3.5.

A final point about stock is that the closing stock for one period becomes the opening stock for the next period. If a factory values its stock at the close of business on 31 January, the figure determined will be the closing stock for January and will also represent the stock available ready to start work on 1 February. Thus January's closing stock figure is the opening stock figure for February.

Value of the Work in Progress

A further complication in the period cost report is that for most factories at the beginning and end of periods, there will be some partially completed garments in the factory. Thus the costs for any period will include costs relating to completing garments started in the previous period and starting garments that will not be completed until the next period. This is known as *work in progress,* and it is customary to value it at the end of each period. Different factories have different methods for valuing the work in progress, but essentially the partly completed garments are counted at different stages of production and a value is placed on them representing their material content and other costs incurred to get them to that stage of completion.

To simplify this, factories will break the factory down into stages—all garments at stage 1 are 10 per cent complete, at stage 2 are 20 per cent complete, at stage 3 are 30 per cent complete and so on. The valuation of the work in progress at the end of one period becomes the value of the opening work in progress for the next period. The period cost report is usually adjusted for the value of the work in progress, and this adjustment is made to the production cost.

Work-in-Progress Adjustment

The work-in-progress adjustment is done as follows:

prime cost

+

production overheads

+

opening value of the work in progress

−

closing value of the work in progress

=

production cost

Period-End Adjustments

As already mentioned, the object of the period cost report is to show the costs for that period. We have seen that this may mean adjusting the report for the value of stocks of direct materials and work in progress. However, other costs are also often adjusted to make them reflect the cost for the period in question. For example, business rates in the UK are usually paid in two halves, one in April and one October. The payment for business rates in April covers the business through until the end of September. The period cost report for each month contains business rates appropriate for only one month.

Example

A business has received its property insurance account for the coming year. It is £4,800, to be paid immediately, and will cover the business from January to December.

When property insurance as a cost is put into the monthly period cost report it will appear as £400 each month (£4,800/12). When the payment is made is not the issue; it is the period for which the cost is incurred that is important.

There now follows a more detailed example of a period cost report. You should consider the data and then look at the report in Table 3.6 to see how it has been analysed. Note how the analysis follows the elements of cost.

The following costs for the month of January were recorded for Alpha Garments Ltd.

Factory wages and salaries

- Cutters: £58,100
- Fusing press operators: £4,320
- Sewing machinists: £134,100
- Press room: £29,200
- Packing: £8,045
- Supervisors: £13,700
- Work study: £3,575
- Cleaning: £8,344
- Factory management: £12,800

Direct materials

- Stocks at start of the period: £178,800
- Stocks at the close of the period: £215,000
- Purchased in the period: £575,000
- Carriage inwards: £5,960

Business rates (2/3 factory): £27,000
Power, light and heat (2/3 factory): £36,000
Insurance (3/4 factory): £16,000
Sales and administration salaries: £63,000
Telephone, postage and stationery: £5,060
Interest on loans and overdrafts: £5,660
Distribution costs: £11,600

Depreciation

- Factory machinery: £20,800
- Factory furniture and fittings: £5,500
- Office furniture and equipment: £3,800

Value of the work in progress

- At the start of the period: £12,660
- At the end of the period: £14,300

TABLE 3.6 Alpha Garments Ltd period cost report—January 20XX

Direct materials	£	£	£
Opening stock		178,800	
Add purchases		575,000	
Add carriage inwards		5,960	
		759,760	
Less closing stock		215,000	
Cost of materials used			**544,760**
Direct labour			
Cutters		58,100	
Fusing press operators		4,320	
Sewing machinists		134,100	
Press room		29,200	
Packing		8,045	
Direct labour cost			**233,765**
Direct expenses			—
Prime cost			**778,525**
Production overhead			
Supervisors	13,700		
Work study	3,575		
Cleaning	8,344		
Factory management	12,800		
Indirect labour cost		38,419	
Business rates		18,000	
Power, light & heat		24,000	
Insurance		12,000	
Depreciation:			
Machinery	20,800		
Furniture and fittings	5,500		
		26,300	

Continued

TABLE 3.6 *(Continued)*

Direct materials	£	£	£
Production overhead cost			**118,719**
			897,244
Add opening work-in-progress			12,660
			909,904
Less closing work-in-progress			14,300
Production cost			**895,604**
Distribution costs		11,600	
Sales and admin salaries		63,000	
Office business rates		9,000	
Heat light & power		12,000	
Insurance		4,000	
Telephone, postage & stationery		5,060	
Depreciation on office furniture		3,800	
Interest on loan and overdrafts		5,660	
Nonproduction overheads			**114,120**
Total cost			**781,484**

Exercises and Activities

1. From the data in Exercise Table 3.1, prepare a period cost statement for Bern Heart Fashions for the month of August analysed over the elements of cost.
2. From the data in Exercise Table 3.2 relating to spring garments for the month of May, prepare a detailed analysed period cost report.
3. From the details in Exercise Table 3.3 relating to direct materials for a manufacturer, produce a report, analysed over each of the stock lines carried by the manufacturer, showing the total opening stock, total purchases for the month, total closing stock and total cost of the materials consumed in the month.

EXERCISE TABLE 3.1

	£
Direct materials purchased	86,700
Cutting room wages	2,300
Sewing room wages	3,500
Press and finishing wages	2,580
Depreciation of factory equipment	350
Depreciation of office equipment	230
Factory supervisors' wages	3,800
Heat, light & power (3/4 factory)	4,200
Insurances (3/4 factory)	250
Administration salaries	2,680
Opening stock of direct materials	2,500
Opening value of work-in-progress	4,250
Closing stock of direct materials	2,800
Closing value of work-in-progress	4,350
Bank charges	120

EXERCISE TABLE 3.2

	£
Opening value of work-in-progress	5,600
Closing value of work-in-progress	6,200
Opening stock of direct materials	7,800
Closing stock of direct materials	9,200
Purchases of direct materials in May	88,000
Carriage inwards for May	230
Returns of direct materials	340
Bank charges and interest	420
Depreciation:	
Office furniture and equipment	120
Factory machinery, furniture & fittings	1,500
Factory supervisors' wages	4,500
Cleaning costs (3/4 factory)	6,400
Sewing machinists' wages	8,600
Cutting room wages	4,400
Press & finishing wages	3,200
Administration wages	2,250
Rent and business rates (80% factory)	5,600
Insurances (80% factory)	250
Postage and stationery	380
Sundry expenses factory	130

EXERCISE TABLE 3.3 October

	£		£
Purchases for the month:		**Closing stock at 31 October:**	
Grey poly cotton	3,500	Grey poly cotton	480
Blue denim	4,200	Blue denim	1,200
Plain calico	2,500	Plain calico	860
White cotton	2,500	White cotton	1,400
Interlining	1,600	Blue cotton	1,250
Buttons	680	Interlinings	2,250
Thread	1,200	Buttons	340
Opening stock at 1 October:		Thread	250
Grey poly cotton	320	Zips	380
Blue denim	2,100	Carriage inwards costs for October:	
Plain calico	2,200	On grey poly cotton	125
White cotton	2,100	On blue denim	80
Blue cotton	1,350		
Interlinings	3,400		
Buttons	1,050		
Thread	860		
Zips	380		

Further Reading

Russell, D., Patel, A., and Wilkinson-Riddle, G. (2002), *Cost Accounting: An Essential Guide,* Harlow: Prentice Hall.

4

PRODUCT COST—JOB COSTING

Introduction

This chapter seeks to explain the costing for individual jobs of work passing through the factory. It is based on the elements of cost and introduces the concept of overhead absorption into costing. By the end of the chapter the student should be able to understand the principles of job costing and be able to produce job costs from given information.

What Is Job Costing?

Job costing is the system of costing jobs of work passing through the factory. Thus if a factory is approached by a retailer to make a quantity of garments, then it is by job costing that the manufacturer can see what it will cost to make the 'job' of garments and see if he can make any profit based on the contract price offered.

The job cost is built up based on the elements of cost considered in the earlier chapters. The principle is to build up the cost of the job starting with the direct materials cost, then the direct labour cost and then the direct expenses (if there are any). This then gives the prime cost of the job. To this is added a 'share' of both the production overheads and the non-production overheads. This traditional system of building up the cost is known as *absorption costing*, and the share of the overheads allocated to each job are known as the *overheads absorbed*.

This system of job costing is illustrated in Figure 4.1.

Treatment of the Direct Costs

With the direct costs, direct materials, direct labour and direct expenses, actual cost is used as far as possible. Thus with the direct materials in garment manufacture the actual cost of the fabrics, linings, threads, buttons, zips and other materials that form the garment is used.

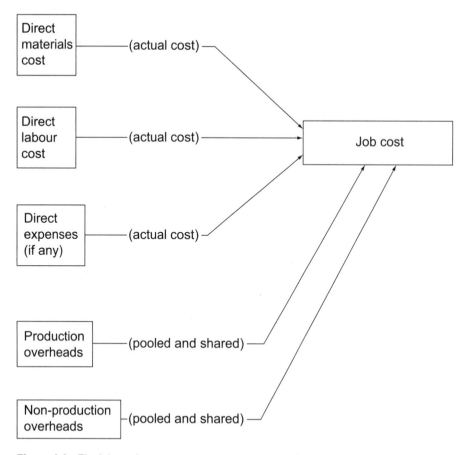

Figure 4.1   The job costing process.

The amount of fabric required per garment is taken from the lay plans; where computerized lay planning is used the computer will give an accurate figure for fabric per garment.

Example

A factory making a job of 20,000 dresses has done its lay plan, and it shows an average fabric usage of 1.25 metres at the standard width. The fabric was purchased for £2.30 per metre, thus the fabric cost in this job will be as follows:

$$1.25 \times 20{,}000 \times £2.30 = £2{,}500.30$$

Other direct materials used to make the garment will also be costed using the actual cost of those materials. There may have to be some estimation in this, for example, with the thread there is no easy or accurate way to cost the quantity used on a garment, so the factory will estimate this cost. However, as far as possible the manufacturer will use actual cost for the direct materials. Care needs to be taken with the direct materials to make sure that all the materials used are included in the job cost. This may include the cost of labels and care labelling. Keep in mind that direct materials are likely to represent 50 per cent of the cost of the job.

Similarly, with the direct labour, the wages cost of those operators who make the garments will be the direct labour cost in the job. This is usually based around the time taken to perform the various manufacturing functions—including laying up and cutting, fusing, a range of sewing operations, pressing and in some cases packing the garments. The costs are based around the time taken for the production activities multiplied by the hourly rates of pay. Here an allowance has to be made to take account of operators who work a little faster or slower than others and the fact that all operators may not achieve the best performance at all times. An allowance to cover the employer's contributions to national insurance and possibly pension schemes—known as *on-cost*—may also be included.

Many of the labour operations will be based around what are referred to as *standard minute values* or *SMVs*. These are the standard times for performing that manufacturing process. For a job of garments these times can be totalled, converted to hours and then multiplied by the appropriate wage rate.

Example

A skirt has an allowance of 12 standard minutes (SM) for its sewing operations. The job involves making 20,000 skirts and the current hourly wage rate for a machinist is £6.10; thus the direct labour cost of the sewing operations will be as follows:

$$(12 \text{ SM} \times 20,000)/60 = 4,000 \text{ direct labour hours}$$
$$4000 \times £6.10 = £24,400 = \text{direct labour cost of the sewing operations}$$

In situations where direct expenses arise, such as royalties or specific costs that relate just to that job of garments, these too are costed based on actual cost. These costs are nearly always quoted per garment or per piece, so they are usually easy to cost.

Example

A jeans manufacturer has a job of 20,000 pairs of jeans, and these require a stonewashed finish. The manufacturer does not do the stonewashing in his own factory but subcontracts the work at £0.20 per pair. Thus this direct expense would be as follows:

$$20,000 \times £0.20 = £4,000 = \text{direct expense cost of stone-washing}$$

Treatment of the Overheads

As has been shown in the preceding chapters, the overheads of the business are grouped into two categories, production overheads and nonproduction overheads. A share of both of these needs to be costed in with the costs of each job. The problem with the overheads is that unlike the direct costs, they do not relate to the jobs of work passing through the factory. The overheads are the broader costs of running the factory and the business and tend to relate to periods of time rather than the product passing through the factory. They nonetheless need to be covered in the job costing process.

A further problem with the overheads is that they are not all paid at one time; they are paid at various times during the year—water and electricity quarterly, business rates half-yearly, rent monthly in advance, management salaries monthly in arrears, supervisors' wages weekly, and so on. Thus at stages through the year the full extent of the overheads is not fully known.

To deal with these problems, absorption costing estimates the overheads in advance, usually for the whole year, and then shares them amongst the job on an agreed basis. This sharing process is known as *overhead absorption* or *overhead recovery.*

Absorption of Production Overheads

There are several methods of absorbing the production overheads into the job cost; however, in this text we will consider four common methods that are widely used.

1. In proportion to the output of the units of product—*unit rate*
2. In proportion to the direct labour hours—*direct labour hour rate*
3. In proportion to the direct labour cost—*percentage of direct labour cost*
4. In proportion to the machine running times—*machine hour rate*

Unit Rate

In this method the total production overheads are estimated for the year and divided by the number of estimated garments to be produced in the year. This gives a rate of overhead to be absorbed per unit of output. The calculation can be summarized as follows:

$$\frac{\text{total estimated overheads}}{\text{estimated total units produced}} = \text{overhead rate per units}$$

Example

A garment manufacturer estimates his overheads to be £125,500 for the year and anticipates an output of 48,000 garments in the year. Thus his production overhead absorption rate will be as follows:

$$\frac{£125,500}{48,000} = £2.61$$

Thus for each garment in the jobs the manufacturer will add £2.61 to the cost to cover the production overheads. In a job to make 20,000 skirts the production overhead figure will be as follows:

$$20,000 \times £2.61 = £52,200 \text{ overhead absorbed}$$

This method suffers because not all the garments manufactured are necessarily the same, and some complex garments may spend more time in manufacture than others. However, for the small manufacturer who makes similar products this may prove to be a simple way to absorb the overheads.

Direct Labour Hour Rate

In this method the total production overheads are estimated for the year and are divided by the estimated total direct labour hours for the year. This gives an amount of production overhead to be absorbed for every direct labour hour in the job. The calculation is as follows:

$$\frac{\text{estimated production overhead}}{\text{estimated direct labour hours}} = \text{direct labour hour rate}$$

Example

A manufacturer estimates his production overheads to be £125,500 for the year and that there will be 19,600 direct labour hours in the year. The calculation of the direct labour hour rate will be as follows:

$$\frac{£125,500}{19,600} = £6.40$$

Thus in a job where the direct labour hours amount to 4,020, the overhead cost to be absorbed into the job cost will be as follows:

$$4,020 \times £6.40 = £25,728 \text{ overhead absorbed}$$

Percentage of Direct Labour Cost

This is a variation on the direct labour hour rate method. The divisor is the estimated direct labour cost rather than the estimated direct labour hours. In situations where the direct wages are the same across the factory or manufacturing department, the result should be similar. The calculation of the percentage of direct labour cost will be as follows:

$$\frac{\text{estimated production overhead}}{\text{estimated direct labour cost}} \times 100 = \text{percentage of direct labour cost}$$

Example

A manufacturer estimates his production overheads to be £125,500 for the year and estimates that the direct labour cost will be £88,200 for the year. Thus the percentage to be used in absorbing the overheads will be as follows:

$$\frac{£125,500}{£88,200} \times 100 = 142.3\%$$

The percentage, 142.3 per cent, is applied to the direct labour cost in the job to obtain the amount of production overhead to be absorbed in the job cost.

Machine Hour Rate

This method of absorbing the production overheads lends itself to factories or manufacturing departments that are largely automated, where the throughput of the product is not controlled by the operator. An automated fusing section or an automated cutting operation might be good examples. In this method the number of machine hours, i.e. the machine running time, is used in the computation of the overhead absorption rate. The calculation of the machine hour rate is as follows:

$$\frac{\text{estimated production overheads}}{\text{total estimated machine hours}} = \text{machine hour rate}$$

Example

A clothing manufacturer has a fusing section that is largely automated. The production overheads in this section are estimated to be £42,500 for the year and the machine running time to be 2,000 hours for the year. Thus the machine hour rate is as follows:

$$\frac{£42,500}{2,000} = £21.25$$

Thus the rate of £21.25 per machine hour will be applied to each job that requires fusing work.

Cost Centres

Whilst it may be possible to calculate an overhead absorption rate for the whole factory, doing so would be unusual in all but very small operations. Most manufacturing units will be broken down into production sections or departments known as *production cost centres*. Each production cost centre will have its own overhead absorption rate, calculated as shown earlier and based on the estimated overheads in that cost centre. This will normally include a share of 'service overheads' like cleaning, maintenance, store keeping, canteen services and the like.

Following are the advantages of having cost centre-based overhead absorption rates:

- They enable a more accurate approach to the costing of overheads in the job costs.
- They allow the factory to use a range of methods of calculating the overhead absorption rates, choosing the ones most suitable for the department concerned.
- Not all jobs necessarily pass through every cost centre; thus only those overheads applicable to the job are absorbed in the job cost.

Absorption of Non-Production Overheads

The non-production overheads represent a much smaller proportion of the overhead cost, but over an annual period they still need to be accounted for in the job costing. Bear in mind that though these costs are a much smaller proportion of the overheads, they are still significant, and in larger companies that tend to have larger administrative structures, the non-production overheads may be very much higher.

The treatment of the non-production overheads in the job costing is to add a small percentage to the production cost of each job. This percentage varies considerably with the size of the business, 2 per cent or 3 per cent in a small business to between 12 per cent and 15 per cent in very large organizations. In theory, by estimating the non-production overheads for the year and taking them as a percentage of the estimated total production cost for the year, the percentage can be calculated as follows:

$$\frac{\text{estimated non-production overheads}}{\text{estimated production cost}} \times 100$$

Example

A manufacturer estimates that his non-production overheads for a year will be £89,350 and his estimated total production costs for the year will be £1,778,000. Thus the absorption of non-production overheads will be based on the following percentage:

$$\frac{£89,350}{£177,8000} \times 100 = 5\%$$

Thus 5 per cent of production costs will be added to each job cost to represent the absorption of the non-production overheads. However, because the absorption of the non-production overheads tends to be a bit arbitrary, some businesses just use a standard percentage; others do not try to absorb the non-production overheads.

Example of a Job Cost

Let us now take an example of a job of garments to be made in a factory. Firstly, the extent of the job and the costs will be collated, and from this we can compile a job cost sheet.

The Job

The job is to produce 50,000 pairs of jeans in a range of sizes. The costing is to include all the materials, packing labels, direct labour and stone washing and appropriate production and nonproduction overheads.

Direct materials

Main fabric: denim—1.285 metres per pair @ £1.80 per metre
Thread: allow £0.05 per pair
Zips: £0.50 per pair
Button studs: £0.03 each; one per pair
Labels: £5.00 per thousand
Cardboard packers: £5.00 per thousand

Direct labour

The job requires three staff to work for 8 hours in laying up and cutting.
The sewing operations take 12 SM per garment.
The press and pack operations take 0.8 SM per garment.

Direct labour rates

Cutting room: £7.20 per hour
Sewing operations: £5.80 per hour
Press and pack: £5.75 per hour

Direct expenses

Stonewashing: Contracted out at £50 per thousand items

Production overheads

Overhead absorption (recovery) is based on the following:

Laying up and cutting: £6.80 per direct labour hour
Sewing operations: 200% of the direct labour cost
Press and pack: 180% of the direct labour cost

Non-production overheads

Overhead absorption (recovery) is based on 5 per cent of the production cost of the job.

Table 4.1 shows the job cost sheet for the 50,000 pairs of jeans order broken down over the elements of cost. At the bottom of the sheet is the total cost, i.e. the cost of producing this order based on the estimated overhead absorption rates. It also shows the unit cost of the job, i.e. the cost on average of making one pair of jeans in the order.

$$\text{unit cost} = \frac{\text{total job cost}}{\text{garments produced}}$$

$$= \frac{£349,355.29}{50,000} = £6.99$$

Different manufacturers may lay out the costs differently, and clearly this lends itself to a computer spreadsheet model. Table 4.1 illustrates the principles to be adopted. Similarly the wage rates, including the on-costs of employment, may be higher and vary among different employers, but the principles are illustrated here.

Over- and Underabsorption of Overheads

We have demonstrated in this chapter that we treat overheads in the product costing by absorbing them based on a predetermined rate. This will entail estimating the overheads in advance, which for an established business should not be a major problem and if done with

TABLE 4.1 Job cost sheet: Jeans, 50,000 pairs

		£p	£p
Direct materials			
Fabric	1.285 × £1.80 × 50,000	115,650.00	
Thread	£0.05 × 50,000	2,500.00	
Zips	£0.50 × 50,000	25,000.00	
Button studs	£0.03 × 50,000	1,500.00	
Labels	£5 × 50	250.00	
Card Packer	£5 × 50	250.00	
			145,150.00
Direct labour			
Cutting room	3 × 8 × £7.20	172.80	
Sewing room	[(12 × 50,000)/60] × £5.80	58,000.00	
Press & pack	[(0.8 × 50,000)/60] × £5.75	3,833.33	
			62,006.13
Direct expenses			
Stonewashing	£50 × 50		**2,500.00**
Production overheads			
Cutting room	3 × 8 × £6.80	163.20	
Sewing room	200% of £58,000	116,000.00	
Press & pack	180% of £3,833.33	6,899.99	
			123,063.19
Production cost			**332,719.32**
Non-production overhead	5% of £332,719.32		**16,635.97**
Total cost			**£349,355.29**
Unit cost	£349,355.29/50,000		**£6.99**

care can be reasonably accurate. However, it is likely at the end of the year that the overheads incurred will not exactly match those absorbed in the product costing.

The overheads absorbed might exceed the actual overheads costs—*overabsorption*—or the overheads absorbed might be lower than the actual overheads cost—*underabsorption*.

The over- and underabsorption will feature in the profit and loss account for the business. Overabsorption increases the profit for the year and underabsorption reduces it. Clearly underabsorption needs to be kept to a minimum in that it reduces the business's anticipated year-end profit and may lead to the acceptance of unviable work—remember, profit margins in clothing manufacture are slim. However, although overabsorption increases the year-end profit, it may result in lost work in that job costs may not be competitive.

Process Costing

Process costing is a form of unit costing, or establishing the cost of one garment. This approach was mentioned in Chapter 3, where it was suggested that the total cost for the period could be divided by the garments produced in the period to give an average unit cost. Clothing manufacturers that continually produce the same product sometimes use this approach, and these manufacturers are all very similar—a shirt factory would be a good example. In such situations the management uses the unit cost or process cost as the guide for making acceptance decisions.

The manufacturer has to take care in accounting for the work in progress in such systems, and an appropriate allowance needs to be made for this. One method is to take the total costs for the period and divide by that number by the completed garments plus the work in progress converted into whole garments (see Table 4.2).

TABLE 4.2

Total costs for the period	£100,000
Complete garments produced	25,000
Part garments: 1,000 20% complete (= 200) 1,000 50% complete (= 500) 1,000 75% complete (= 750) Work-in-progress expressed as complete garment	1,450
Total output for the period	26,450
Process cost per garment	£3.78

Example

You can see in Table 4.2 that the work in progress at the end of the period is expressed in terms of completeness—thus 1,000 garments that are 20 per cent complete represent 200 complete garments. The notional numbers of complete garments are then added to the actually complete garments to give the divisor used in calculating the process cost. In the example in Table 4.2 it is as follows:

$$\frac{£100,000}{26,450} = £3.78 \text{ per garment}$$

1. Mercia Fashions

Mercia Fashions does its job costing based on the following rates shown in Exercise Table 4.1.

EXERCISE TABLE 4.1

	Cutting	Fusing	Sewing	Pressing	Packing
Direct labour	£11.05	£6.25	£6.75	£7.15	£6.25
Production overheads	DLHR	MHR	%DLC	DLHR	%DLC
Production overhead rate	£15.20	£6.70	180%	£7.60	150%

Additionally, Mercia Fashions adds 5 per cent of production cost to all jobs to cover the absorption of the nonproduction overheads.

Job to Make 20,000 Ladies' Dresses

Direct materials
The lay plan shows that the average fabric requirement per dress is 1.4 metres at a cost of £5.20 per metre.
Zips: one per garment—£0.45
Buttons: 3 per garment—£0.01 each
Interlining: allow £0.25 per garment
Thread: allow £0.20 per garment

Direct labour
Laying up and cutting will involve three operators for six hours.
Fusing of the whole 20,000 dresses can be done in three machine hours; however, it will involve the operator in four hours of work.
Sewing requires 10 SM per garment.
Pressing requires 0.5 SM per garment.
Packing requires 0.4 SM per garment.
Provide a job cost sheet showing the total job cost and the unit cost.

2. Frankfurt Fashions

Frankfurt Fashions is a clothing manufacturer producing ladies' wear. The factory is organized into three production departments, and each department is a cost centre with a separate overhead absorption rate for absorbing the overheads.

The three departments (cost centres) are cutting, sewing and press/finish. They absorb their production overheads as follows:

Cutting: Machine hour rate
Sewing: Percentage of direct labour cost
Press/Finish: Direct labour hour rate

In addition to the overheads that relate to the production departments there are also some service overheads, such as maintenance, cleaning, and factory personnel, and these are allocated to the production departments. Exercise Table 4.2 details the estimates for the coming financial period.

Calculate the appropriate overhead absorption rates for the production overheads for the factory. The factory also adds 5 per cent to the production cost to cover nonproduction overheads.

EXERCISE TABLE 4.2

	Cutting	Sewing	Press/Finish
Estimated overheads	£24,000	£96,000	£22,000
Service overheads:			
Maintenance	£6,500	£35,600	£6,700
Cleaning	£7,500	£23,400	£6,000
Personnel	£4,500	£25,500	£10,500
Total	£42,500	£180,500	£45,200
Direct labour hours	5,500	18,240	5,000
Machine hours	3,600	—	—
Direct labour cost	£71,000	£114,200	£33,500

3. Offas Fashions Ltd

Offas Fashions Ltd, a garment manufacturer, uses job costing and in the current year is using the wages rates and overheads absorption rates shown in Exercise Table 4.3.

Additionally Offas Fashions Ltd add 5 per cent of production cost to all jobs to cover nonproduction overheads. You are required to produce a total job cost and a unit cost for the following job.

Job No: 1578/003

The job involves making 50,000 pairs of trousers in various sizes, in one fabric.

EXERCISE TABLE 4.3

	Cutting	Sewing	Press/Finish
Estimated overheads	£24,000	£96,000	£22,000
Service overheads:			
Maintenance	£6,500	£35,600	£6,700
Cleaning	£7,500	£23,400	£6,000
Personnel	£4,500	£25,500	£10,500
Total	£42,500	£180,500	£45,200
Direct labour hours	5,500	18,240	5,000
Machine hours	3,600	—	—
Direct labour cost	£71,000	£114,200	£33,500

Direct materials

The lay plan shows that the average fabric requirement per pair of trousers is 1.29 metres, based on a fabric width of 150 cm. The cost of the fabric is £2.75 per metre.

Zips: £0.48 each; one per pair
Waistband lining: allow £0.15 per garment
Fusible interlining: allow £0.20 per garment
Metal hook fasteners: £0.01 each; one per pair
Thread: allow £0.25 per garment

Direct labour

Laying up and cutting will take 3 operators 10 hours, using 28 hours of machine time.
Fusing the whole job can be done in 3 hours of machine time; however this will involve 4 hours of operator time.

4. Wessex Wear Ltd

Wessex Wear Ltd, a garment manufacturer, uses job costing and in the current year is using the wages rates and overheads absorption rates shown in Exercise Table 4.4.

Additionally Wessex Wear Ltd adds 5 per cent of production cost to all jobs to cover nonproduction overheads. You are required to produce a total job cost and a unit cost for the following job.

Job No: 1679/003

The job involves making 25,000 denim skirts in a small range of sizes, in one fabric.

EXERCISE TABLE 4.4

	Cutting	Sewing	Pressing
Direct wage rate (per hour)	£8.75	£4.50	£4.60
Overhead absorption	Direct labour hour rate	Percentage of DLC	Direct labour hour rate
Overhead rate	£10.50	175%	£5.50

Direct materials

The lay plan shows that the average fabric requirement per skirt is 0.85 metres, based on a fabric width of 150 centimetres. The cost of the fabric is £2.45 per metre.

Zips: £0.45 each—one per skirt

Button: £0.01 each—one per skirt

Thread: allow £0.20 per skirt

Direct labour

Laying up and cutting will take three operators 6 hours.

The sewing operations require 9.5 SM per garment.

Pressing requires 0.40 SM.

Direct expenses

Stonewashing and ripping are to be done externally at £0.36 per garment.

Further Reading

Drury, C. (2003), *Cost and Management Accounting: An introduction* (5th edn), London: Thomson Learning.

Drury, C. (2005), *Management Accounting for Business* (3rd edn), London: Thomson Learning.

Drury, C. (2008), *Management and Cost Accounting* (7th edn), London: Thomson Learning.

Horngren, C. T., Sundem, G. L., and Stratton, W. O. (2008), *Introduction to Management Accounting* (14th edn), Harlow: Pearson Prentice Hall.

Lucey, T. (2009), *Costing* (7th edn), London: Cengage Learning.

Russell, D., Patel, A., and Wilkinson-Riddle, G. (2002), *Cost Accounting: An Essential Guide*, Harlow: Prentice Hall.

5

GLOBAL AWARENESS AND NEW MARKETS

Introduction

The next two chapters are not about to argue whether companies should operate in a global context; many of them already do so. The aim is to provide some background to the main topics encountered in off-shore garment costing and production from a practical perspective. These chapters will provide a broad knowledge of the 'rag trade', and the reader is advised to complete the practical exercises to illustrate the points made. Working in this industry is exciting and challenging; what makes it so are the various ways in which companies operate in their bid to dominate the high street. What makes this environment unique is that no two businesses operate in exactly the same way, even though some of the processes are identical.

Jones (2006) provides a background that helps to contextualize the terminology used. He defines the term *supply chain* as companies independent of each other but working towards a common goal (such as producing garments). However, terms such as *clothing, fashion* and *garment* are used in turn and whenever appropriate in a specific context and, unlike in Jones, will not be grouped under one umbrella.

The Global Supply Chain

The global supply chain is in a constant state of flux and encompasses existing key players along with emerging markets. To facilitate the discussion we will split the retail environment into three main categories: high (luxury brands), middle (high street retailers) and low (value retailers and discounters). The economic downturn over the past eighteen months combined with a competitive retail environment means that more than ever, businesses need to demonstrate creative and commercial flair to prosper. Celebrities and instantaneous reports on fashion shows fuel the public's desire for key looks at a fraction of the price. This phenomenon has driven retailers to rethink their distribution strategies at home and globally. In a bid to satisfy consumer demand and in order to survive in this arena, retailers need to react fast and frequently. Key players in the global arena who distribute branded goods step up their marketing campaigns to raise brand awareness and strengthen their position on the market. UK clothing businesses can be considered global by either importing into the home market or distributing internationally. As Jones (2006) points out, "Competition is becoming more global or at least intra-country activity is increasing whether it be measured by trade flows, investment flows or people flows."

One route for expansion that many companies choose is overseas distribution; this cannot be achieved without reputable contacts who understand the local market and are prepared to invest in a marketing strategy.

Barriers and Facilitators in Market-Entry Strategies

Clothing businesses that have plans for growth and expansion might choose to export as part of their strategy. The market-entry strategy will be driven by the size of the business, whether a brand is being distributed, the targeted countries, the objectives of the business and the timing. To enter unknown markets, exporters need to possess an understanding of the marketing environments of the countries in which they wish to operate. One of the popular choices is to seek links with distributors that are already established in their home market. With minimum financial exposure exporters acquire an exclusive insight into the market and are able to overcome obstacles such as culture and language, regulations and logistics.

Exporters will need to strategically devise their market-entry strategy and concentrate on the markets, the products, the positioning and the competitors (Mintzberg et al. 1998). To operate in an international context, exporters must forge alliances with trustworthy foreign partners. This could be a serious business advantage, particularly in an environment where price and quality are of the essence. Dealing with already established intermediaries in an unknown market provides supplementary security to the exporter. However, finding the right partners to be the exporter's 'voice and ears' is not an easy task and clearly comprises a risk which needs to be managed.

Global Communication

The supply chain involves different players: the retailer provides the public with finished goods, the manufacturer or factory (and their suppliers) produces the garments that are sold by the retailers and the agent acts as a middleman between the factories and the retailers. The agents are increasingly cut out of the equation as retailers and manufacturers deal with each other in a bid to maximize profitability and speed up the manufacturing process to have a greater turnover of stock. There are reasons as to why some agents are surviving in this tough climate; their success can be attributed to excellent designs and sampling facilities as well as long-established relationships with retailers, which therefore enables a share of their orders to be offloaded to the agent,

Companies handle issues relating to communications in various ways and develop systems of working with partners overseas by trial and error. Email and mobile phones have facilitated communication but are not the panacea to resolving the language and cultural barriers faced by those dealing in the global arena (whether it be from a manufacturing, agent or retailing perspective). UK suppliers often find their manufacturers struggling with demands for commercial samples that are used to sell the collection given that CAD drawings are no longer acceptable as a sales tool. During the selection process retailers want to see samples that resemble the finished garment. This has led to drastic changes in the way retailers and agents operate: they have set up buying offices and work in partnership with factories in the countries of manufacture, thus resulting in stronger levels of control over the product development and manufacturing processes. These business partnerships are mutually beneficial; as both parties develop a better understanding of each other's culture they strengthen their positions in the marketplace. Some UK businesses cannot afford the expenditure or deem this approach an unviable option; they choose to run the operations remotely, resulting in frequent overseas trips and a greater exposure to risk. Either way there is an indisputable need for timely and accurate supply of information, because any holdback has ramifications over delivery dates.

It is vital in the purchasing function that both the buyer and the supplier fully understand the specifications of the goods involved in the transaction, and therefore communication is the key to success: mistakes are costly and can damage the company's reputation. To optimize turnover it is necessary to have access to up-to-date information on the progress of production along with a full range of samples in accurate quality, size and colour. Failure to provide these will result in poor sales performance and will damage hard-to-establish relationships with retailers.

Purchase Order

The purchase order, or PO (Figure 5.1), is a contractual agreement between the purchaser and the supplier. Its purpose is to provide as much information about the product purchased prior to the start of production. Its layout and contents are subject to variations but generally it will state the following:

- Order number and account number.
- Price per garment in the negotiated currency.
- Total order quantity.
- Size specification reference number, which might refer to a basic size chart that can be amended accordingly. If it is a repeat order the reference number will be that of the initial order.

PURCHASE ORDER FORM (PO FORM)			
SIZE SPECIFICATION REFERENCE NUMBER:			
SUPPLIER NAME:	RAISED BY:		ISSUE DATE:
CUSTOMER NAME:	ORDER NO:		ACCOUNT NO:
TO BE DELIVERED TO:	DESPATCH DATE:		BUY PRICE (per garment):
STYLE DESCRIPTION:	TOTAL ORDER QUANTITY:		STYLE NO:
ADDITIONAL COMMENTS:			
SHIPMENT SCHEDULE / COMMENTS / SPECIAL INSTRUCTIONS:			
FREIGHT FORWARDER:			
PACKAGING DETAILS:			
NOMINATED SUPPLIERS FOR HANGERS / LABELS / STICKERS / PACKAGING:			
CUSTOMER REFERENCE NUMBER:			
PACKING LIST / ASSORTMENT:			

SIZES:	PRODUCT CODE:	QTY:	VALUE:	CUSTOMER REF:

Figure 5.1 Example of a purchase order for goods shipped to the United Kingdom.

- Style number—relates to the product stated in the PO, whereas the order number could include several items in the collection, each with its own order number.
- Customer reference number—if an agent is acting on behalf of a retailer, it will be necessary to stipulate their reference number.
- Brief description of the product—sometimes a front and back sketch of the item is attached to the PO.
- Supplier name—name of the manufacturer producing the goods.
- Issue date—the date the PO has been raised.
- Name of the person who has raised the PO.
- Name of the customer (it could be either an agent or a retailer).
- Freight forwarder—the role of the forwarder is to ensure the smooth transit of goods internationally.
- Delivered to—specifies the final destination.
- Despatch date—indicates when the goods will be ready to be shipped.
- Packaging details—states how the garment should be presented, for example on a hanger, in a poly bag, with care label, size label, back neck label, swing tickets, etc. Positioning of these labels is also specified.
- Nominated suppliers—some retailers may want to use specific suppliers for their hangers, labels, swing tickets and hanger stickers and as such the PO states where these should be purchased from and their reference numbers.
- Packing list/assortment—once the production is complete, goods will need to be packed in marked cartons and occasionally inner cartons. The final packing list is usually sent to the customer once the goods are packed and carton numbers have been allocated. Initially the number of pieces per carton, the ratio of sizes and colours is communicated. (You will have an opportunity to calculate the ratio packing in the "Exercise" section at the end of this chapter.)
- Additional comments—can contain information such as fabric and garment testing requirements, factory audits and ethical requirements.

An example of a PO for a product bought from a UK supplier and exported to mainland Europe is shown in Figure 5.2. Similar information to that discussed in Figure 5.1 is required, with additional points relating to pricing and exclusivity to the country to which it is sold.

Lead Times

To insure that garments will be available in store on time, buyers need to calculate how long each process will take. The total amount of time (normally quantified in number of weeks) is the lead time which can be defined as the time required from placement to completion of an order. The word completion is subject to variations: one party might assume that an order is complete once it is packed in a carton ready to be shipped, whilst another might deem the order complete once it is delivered to a given address. It is therefore important to give and receive clear directives at the onset to avoid misunderstandings. Figure 5.3 demonstrates the

PRODUCT INFORMATION SHEET

LOGO / NAME AND CONTACT DETAILS OF THE RETAILER

Company name: _____

Product name: _____

Reference number: _____

1/ PRICE AND AVAILABILITY

Export price list: ❏ €uro   ❏ £   ❏ USD   ❏ Other currency:_____

€0.21 WILL BE ADDED TO THIS PRICE FOR ORDERS WITH HEADER CARD

Discount: _____%

Net price: ❏ €uro   ❏ £   ❏ USD   ❏ Other currency:_____

Valid until: _____   Retail price in your domestic market?
_____

Delivery conditions (Incoterms): _____

Minimum order quantity: _____ pieces

Delivery delay: _____

Will re-orders be: a) Provided from stock   ❏

b) Made to order   ❏

c) Imported to order   ❏

2/ RETAILING OUTSIDE OF THE UK

Item already sold overseas?:   ❏ Yes   ❏ No

To whom?: _____

What is the retail price in the home country?: _____

Exclusivity possible?: ❏ Yes   ❏ No

Exclusivity conditions: _____

Figure 5.2 Example of a purchase order for goods shipped to the United Kingdom and exported to the European Union.

3/ PRODUCT SPECIFICATIONS

Type of packaging: _____

(if polybag: please ensure it carries a warning against risks of suffocation in the specified language and that the thickness of the polybag is <u>above 0.038 mm.</u>)

Dimension of the item with its packaging: _____

Unit weight of the item with its packaging: _____

Age recommended by the manufacturer on the packaging: _____

Multilingual packaging?: _____

Instruction for use in specified language?: _____

If not, can you insert a translation?: _____

Does the packaging bear the green dot?:   ❏ Yes   ❏ No

Minimum quantity for packaging?: _____

CD-rom and program specification for our agency to send you the artwork (for packaging development): _____

4/ SHIPMENTS

Product origin (manufacturing country): _____

Custom identification number: _____

Warehouse address: _____
_____
_____

Port of departure: _____

THE BELOW INFORMATION IS COMPULSORY TO CONSIDER REFERENCING YOUR PRODUCTS: please also indicate the measuring unit (<u>inches/cm/pound or kilogrammes</u>)

Units per master carton: _____

Dimension of a master carton: _____

Weight of a master carton: GROSS _____   NET_____

Volume of a master carton: _____

Quantity per pallet: _____

processes involved to work out lead times in garment production. It is important to note that the lead times will vary according to the processes involved and are pre-agreed at the time of negotiations between the purchaser and the manufacturer.

Purchase orders are raised once the lead times have been agreed between the two parties, who are then bound in a contractual agreement. To further strengthen the legal aspect of the order, a Letter of Credit (LC) is raised by the purchaser to the attention of the manufacturer. An LC is a promise to pay and is raised by the purchaser's bank as a way to

ORDER NUMBER	TOTAL ORDER QUANTITY	ORDER SHIP DATE	CONTRACT DETAILS SENT OUT	SIZE SET SAMPLES RECEIVED AND COMMENTS SENT BACK	LAB DIP RECEIVED AND COMMENTS SENT BACK	ACCESSORIES RECEIVED AND COMMENTS SENT BACK	SIZE SET SAMPLES RECEIVED AND COMMENTS SENT BACK	ACCESSORIES AND TRIMS RECEIVED AND COMMENTS SENT BACK	LABELS, SWING TICKETS AND TRIMS RECEIVED AND COMMENTS SENT BACK	PRE-PRODUCTION SAMPLES RECEIVED AND COMMENTS SENT BACK	PRODUCTION SAMPLES SENDING DATE RECEIVED AND COMMENTS SENT BACK	AQL CARRIED OUT	ETD	VESSEL NAME OR AIR FREIGHT DETAILS	ETA UK	ETA WAREHOUSE
			1	3	4	4	4	4	4	7	8	10	12			

Notes: Numbers indicate weeks.

Figure 5.3 Example of how a twelve-week lead time is calculated.

ensure that the supplier will get paid as long as it does what it has agreed to do. Failure to respect the terms of the PO and the LC will result in penalization or litigation. Depending upon the severity of the problem, common penalties imposed on suppliers are a request for a discount on the agreed price, a demand for goods to be air instead of sea freighted or cancellation of the order.

Figure 5.3 illustrates how a twelve-weeks lead time might be calculated and is not dissimilar to the PO in terms of the information it contains. However, it is not uncommon for the purchaser to reject lab dips or size set samples, which will mean that the supplier has to resubmit the sample for approval. The high street is characterized by quick response, thus underlining the importance of time management. Achievable targets need to be calculated, ensuring that a margin of error is allowed for unforeseen problems, such as delays in production or shipment. The ETD (Estimated Time of Departure), the ETA date (Estimated Time of Arrival) and shipping vessel's name are provided by the freight forwarder, who will endeavour to adhere to these shipment dates.

Critical Path

Once the lead times have been calculated and the PO has been raised, systems need to be implemented to monitor the progress of production. The system is known as *critical path* or *crit path management* and can be defined as a sequence of key deadlines that need to be met to achieve a predetermined delivery date.

Several software packages are available in the marketplace, and therefore the PO's layout is likely to vary in appearance depending on the particular software used. It is a pre-emptive tool used to track the progress of production and can draw attention to shipment delays earlier in the process. The number of columns will reduce or expand depending on the number of features contained within the garment.

The steps involved can be explained as follows:

Week 1: The buyer sends out the order/PO to the supplier; the supplier places the fabric order and starts to produce approval samples in available, not production, fabric and trims.
Week 2: Fabric production starts; the buyer receives the approval samples and comments; the supplier orders trims and accessories to coordinate delivery of fabric, accessories and trims.
Week 3: A Letter of Credit (LC) is opened by the buyer's bank; the buying team comments on the lab dips, trims and accessories.
Weeks 4 and 5: Fabric, trims and accessories are in production.
Week 6: Fabric, trims and accessories are shipped to the supplier. The supplier sends a pre-production sample, in the correct fabric, trims and accessories, to the buyer for comments.
Week 7: The buyer comments on the pre-production sample.
Week 8: The supplier starts the production.

Weeks 9 and 10: Garment production continues.
Week 11: Production finishes, and inspection is carried out to ensure that garments are of an acceptable quality level (AQL) (the percentage is variable).
Week 12: The supplier checks the production sample and allows the shipment of goods.

The critical path will extend beyond twelve weeks to allow for transit (duration will vary pending upon the country of manufacture and freight method) and custom clearance.

The empty squares would normally be filled with comments recording in as much detail as possible the progress of production.

Vertical integration is increasingly popular as a way to reduce lead times and transport costs as well as provide better control of the supply-chain management. It can be adopted by retailers and manufacturers and broadly means that as many processes as possible are undertaken in-house. For example, a retailer's strategy to overcome difficulties with global manufacturing might be to market, design, dye, cut, sew, finish and distribute garments directly into stores. The strategy simplifies communication and mitigates risk.

Exercise

When raising a PO, the buyer needs to specify how many pieces are to be packed in each carton and to what ratio. It will also be necessary to specify how the goods are to be packaged individually: hangers, poly bags, labelling and swing tickets.

Consider the following order and calculate the quantities per size and per colour:

Embroidered T-shirt
Reference: 0045L
Quantity: 3,600 pieces
Colours: Navy, white, black, red
Sizes: 10, 12, 14, 16
Ratio:

Navy and red: 1 : 1 : 1 : 1
White and black: 1 : 2 : 2 : 1

Recommended Reading

Jones, R. (2006), *The Apparel Industry* (2nd edn), Oxford : Blackwell.
Mintzberg, H., Quinn, J. B., and Ghoshal, S. (1998), *The Strategy Process: Revised European Edition* (2nd edn), Harlow: Prentice Hall. http://www.ethicalfashionforum.com (accessed December 2009).

6

PRODUCT COST WHEN SOURCING

Introduction

Garments mass-produced for the high street are often embellished with prints, embroideries and intricate finishing details which can cause varying degrees of complications during the manufacturing process. These intricate details, along with the fabric costs, represent a large portion of the total cost of garments and need to be closely monitored. The high street is fickle and driven by consumers' search for designer looks at a fraction of the designer cost, which necessitates a quick response from retailers in order to maximize financial gain from these latest trends. The global sourcing strategy which aims to find and evaluate suitable manufacturers is therefore a driver to achieving sales targets and increased profit margins.

Global Sourcing

The shift of production from the UK to overseas over past decades has been significant to the range and variety of products available in the high street. Low labour production costs have enabled retailers to increase profitability whilst offering a broader product range to the customers. Low labour cost is not a panacea to struggling businesses, and there are advantages and disadvantages to be mindful of. As well as labour cost, the main advantages to overseas production are the capacity to mass manufacture and the competition amongst factories which acts as a stimulus. As well as the cultural differences, some of the disadvantages are lengthy travelling; communication within different time zones; freight and shipping costs; legal and administrative costs and the risk of copyright infringements, particularly when distributing a brand name. The technological advancements of recent years can be compared to the progress made during the industrial revolution; global sourcing is far easier to manage with information technology at our fingertips. With the exception of CMT (cut, make and trim) factories, small design companies and bespoke tailors, clothing manufacture in the UK has dwindled as few have managed to survive overseas competition. Value retailers have set up trends for mass manufacturing and selling at rock bottom prices and have thereby put pressure onto other smaller retailers to find cheaper sources of supply despite lacking the buying power to apply economies of scale to the negotiation tables. One is drawn to reflect upon the future of UK manufacturing and its possible revival in light of consumers' interest in 'green' fashion (ecologically sound, organic, fair-trade, sustainable, ethical) and the media coverage it receives. Retailers are under pressure from the consumer to offer such products, which could spur a manufacturing renaissance in the UK: basic garments classified under the green umbrella could be produced in the home market and retail at a higher price point, which would redress the balance and expose retailers to less risk by not having all their garments produced overseas.

Range Planning

The rapid changes in fashion trends and their effect on the retail environment have been discussed. They point to the need for quick response to meet consumers' demands, which would imply lack of forward planning from the part of retailers. To take advantage of unforeseen trends, to repeat buy successful products or to add new products to the range, retailers hold back funds, known as open-to-buy. The development of a product range is time critical, necessitates in-depth research into fashion trends and above all should be designed to appeal to loyal customers whilst attracting new ones.

Designers strive to develop new ideas twelve months ahead of the season and are often asked to rework best-sellers. As well as reading glossy magazines and browsing the internet for the latest podcasts of catwalk shows, designers gather trends by attending trade shows, subscribing to forecasting catalogues and Web sites such as WGSN. With new ideas in mind they travel within the UK and abroad to carry out competition and directional shopping (comp shop), which entails purchasing samples representative of the types of products proposed for the oncoming season. A range plan meeting is scheduled to kick-start the selection process whereby bought samples, mood boards, CAD drawings and illustrations are reviewed by the buying and product development teams. The outcome of the meeting will necessitate further work from the design team until the range is signed off and budgets have been allocated to purchase the range.

Buyers, operations managers and product developers (depending on the structure of the business) will establish the country of manufacture, which is determined by the product type, and decide which factories will be invited to tender for the business. In preparation for the negotiations that will take place during the buying trip, it is necessary to establish, for each garment, the order quantity, the buying price, the retail selling price and the lead times. Once prices have been agreed with the supplier, a request for sales samples is made in preparation for the range preview. Purchase orders will be raised immediately: the production process will start and be monitored using the critical path.

Factories

Before placing orders with a factory overseas it is necessary to possess an in-depth knowledge of the politics, economics and infrastructure of the chosen country. Frequent monitoring and rating of performance will take place. Buyers will, with experience, acquire a portfolio of factories which will have been trialled and tested over the years. However several key issues are under scrutiny:

- Lead times: If orders were placed in previous seasons, an analysis of adherence to the delivery schedule will take place.
- Pricing: To achieve targets, prices need to be maintained.
- Quality: Were the garments produced according to the expected standards, and if not, what measures were put in place to rectify problems?
- Product type: Factories tend to specialize in specific product areas and need to maintain the leading edge over competitors.
- Ethical trading: High street retailers have got a responsibility to ensure that working conditions in the global supply chain are in accordance with the code of labour practice and as such should audit the factories regularly.
- Sampling: Once orders are raised sales, size set, preproduction and production samples are requested to ensure adherence to size, fit and quality standards.

Shipping and Incoterms

The shipment of goods on an international scale is a complicated and laborious process which usually involves a great number of administrative, consular, fiscal and custom formalities. Businesses will either possess an import/export department or use a freight forwarder to deal with formalities. Freight forwarders play an integral part in the transportation process and as such will provide the documentation for transportation, work out best routing and book the freight on appropriate vessels, deal with customs officers, liaise with the shipping agent and ensure that the information is transmitted to the purchaser for better control of the lead times. They also provide help and advice on freight cost, documentation and regulations; book space with freight carriers; oversee customs clearance; book and pack containers and organize cargo insurance, all of which come with additional cost. In time-critical situations, their services are often invaluable.

Incoterms refers to International Commercial Terms, which were first published in 1936 (see www.iccwbo.org/incoterms). Knowledge of these terms is important to import and export agents—those working in the shipping department of a fashion business. Whilst many students will not follow this career path, knowledge of Incoterms can prove a useful asset. They are revised periodically to keep up with international trade needs and can be defined as terms used to define the role of the seller and that of the buyer in the planning of

PRODUCT COST WHEN SOURCING

transportation. Incoterms clarify when the ownership of the goods takes place. There are eleven terms, and these are illustrated in Figure 6.1. The points to remember are as follows:

- Terms beginning with E: Seller's responsibility fulfilled when goods are ready to leave their facility.
- Terms beginning with F: Seller does not pay for the primary cost of shipping.
- Terms beginning with C: Seller pays for shipping.
- Terms beginning with D: Seller's responsibility ends when goods arrive at a specific point.

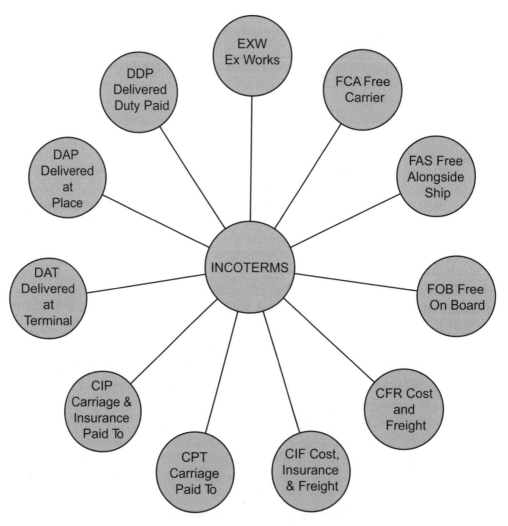

Figure 6.1 List of the International Commercial Terms devised by the International Chamber of Commerce. (www.iccwbo.org/incoterms)

Not all of the thirteen terms will be used in the fashion industry. Illustrated in Figure 6.2 are the most commonly used Incoterms and are briefly discussed below:

- Ex Works (EXW): The seller's responsibility ends at his premises; it represents the minimum responsibility for the seller. The buyer has to bear all the costs and risks involved in taking the goods from the seller's premises.
- Free Carrier (FCA): The seller delivers the goods, cleared for export, to the carrier (this applies to any form of transport: road, rail, sea air) nominated by the buyer at the named place. The chosen delivery has an impact on the obligations of loading and unloading the goods at that place.
- Free Alongside Ship (FAS): The seller delivers when the goods are placed alongside the vessel at the named port of shipment. The buyer has to bear costs and risks from that point onwards. Used for sea or inland waterway transport.
- Free On Board (FOB): The seller delivers when the goods pass the ship's rail at the named port of shipment. The buyer has to bear costs and risks from that point onwards. The seller has to clear the goods for export. Used for sea or inland waterway transport.
- Cost and Freight (CFR): The seller delivers when the goods pass the ship's rail in the port of shipment. The seller pays for the costs and freight to bring the goods to the named port of destination. Other risks such as loss or damage to the goods are the buyer's responsibility. The seller clears the goods for export. Used for sea or inland waterway transport.
- Cost, Insurance and Freight (CIF): The seller delivers when the goods pass the ship's rail in the port of shipment. The seller clears the goods for export and pays the costs and freight to bring the goods to the named port of destination. Other risks, such as loss or damage to the goods,

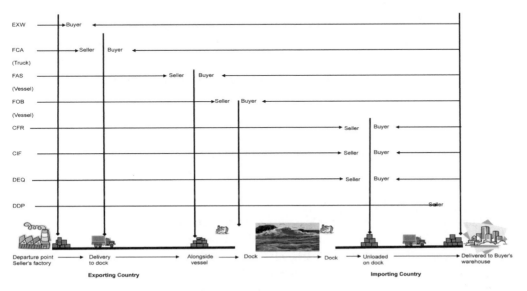

Figure 6.2 Diagram of the most commonly used Incoterms.

are the buyer's responsibility. The seller pays for the insurance on the maritime trip. Used for sea or inland waterway transport.

- Delivered Duty Paid (DDP): The seller delivers the goods to the buyer, not cleared for import and not unloaded from any arriving means of transport at the named place of destination. The seller has to bear all the costs and risks involved in bringing the goods into the country of destination. DDP represents the maximum obligation for the seller. This term may be used for any mode of transport (sea, air, road, rail).

Exercise: Overseas Cost Sheets

Given that we have discussed the processes involved in sourcing garments in a global context, this exercise illustrates how one might set out to calculate costs from a non-UK perspective (see Exercise Table 6.1). Had the garments been manufactured in the UK, the costing sheet would focus mainly on production and nonproduction overheads, not on rates of exchange (ROE), freight cost, packaging and testing costs.

The exercise you are advised to carry out emulates a scenario where garments have been purchased from the Far East in US dollars and will be sold in euros to a distributor. The costing sheet is prepared prior to the buying trip and in preparation for negotiations—once prices are negotiated and POs raised, it can be revised to give a true reflection of margins. It is common to allocate estimated costs for freight, labels, swing tickets, packaging and testing. The cost sheet contains for each item (from left to right) a style number, PO number, total order quantity, shipping/freight date, date of delivery to the customer's warehouse, price the garment is sold at in euros and its conversion into UK pounds, factory name, buying price in US dollars and its conversion into UK pounds, labelling/packaging/testing cost in UK pounds, freight/shipping cost in UK pounds, total garment cost in UK pounds, gross profit per garment in UK pounds, percentage margin per garment, turnover the item generates in UK pounds and total gross profit the item generates in UK pounds. Rates of exchange have been set at 1 UK£ equals 1.65 US$ and 1.45 euros.

The cost sheet contains numbers in bold ranging from 1 to 11 that have been inserted at the tops of columns or inside individual cells to provide step-by-step guidance on how to calculate the costing sheet; see the following detailed working outs.

- **1** (sell price £) = (sell price euro) / 1.45
- **2** (£ buy price) = (US$ buy price) × 1.65
- **3** (total garment cost £) = (£ buy price) + (pack & test costs £) + (freight cost £)
- **4** (gross profit £ per garment) = (sell price £) – (total garment cost £)
- **5** (% margin) = (gross profit £ per garment) / (sell price £)
- **6** (total sales £) = (order quantity) × (sell price £)
- **7** (total gross profit £) = (gross profit £ per garment) × (order quantity)
- **8** (order quantity) = all five order quantities are added up and totalled

EXERCISE TABLE 6.1

							1			2			3	4	5	6	7
STYLE No	P/O No	STYLE DESCRIPTION	ORDER QUANTITY	SHIP DATE	DELIVERY DATE	SELL PRICE EURO	SELL PRICE £	FACTORY NAME	US$ BUY PRICE	£ BUY PRICE	PACK & TEST COSTS £	FREIGHT COST £	TOTAL GMENT COST £	GROSS PROFIT £ / GMENT	% GMENT MARGIN	TOTAL SALES £	TOTAL GROSS PROFIT £
		EMBROIDED BLOUSE	7600	30-Jun	25-Aug	5.59		D	3.50		£0.44	£0.35					
		PEARL BUTTON BLOUSE	3000	30-Jun	25-Aug	3.99		C	2.20		£0.44	£0.35					
		BOW BLOUSE	4800	30-Jun	25-Aug	7.00		C	3.50		£0.44	£0.35					
		GATHERED HEM BLOUSE	2000	30-Jun	25-Aug	7.25		C	4.00		£0.44	£0.35					
		APPLIQUE BLOUSE	5600	30-Jun	25-Aug	5.75		D	3.75		£0.44	£0.35					
TOTAL			8												11	9	10

DEPARTMENT OVERALL TOTAL % MARGIN

ROE   1.65   US $

ROE   1.45   EURO

- **9** (total sales £) = all five total sales £ are added up and totalled
- **10** (total gross profit £) = all five total gross profit £ are added up and totalled
- **11** represents the department overall total % margin for all five items = (all five % margin added up and totalled) / 5

Recommended Reading

Cooklin, G. (2006), *Introduction to Clothing Manufacture,* revised by Hayes, S. G., and McLoughlin, J., Oxford: Blackwell Science.

www.export911.com

www.ethicaltrade.org

www.iccwbo.org/incoterms/id3045/index.html [accessed December 2009]

Glossary of Terms

Agent: Intermediary party between the purchaser and the manufacturer

CAD: Computer-aided design

Critical path or crit path: A sequence of key deadlines that need to be met to achieve a predetermined delivery date

Factory audit: To ensure that garments are produced in line with the code of labour practice (ETI Base Code of labour practice; see www.ethicaltrade.org), retailers carry out checks in terms of the workers' welfare, their working environment, the working order of machinery and the compliance to agreed terms

Lab dips: Swatches of fabrics which have been dyed to the buyer's request and which need to match either a Pantone shade or a swatch of fabric which has been cut off a bought sample. Normally several dips will be offered for the buyer to select from. Swatches of fabric are sent to the buyer for colour approval before the bulk fabric is dyed and finished.

Lead time: The time required between the initiation of a process and the completion of that process.

Purchase order (PO): A contract between two parties finalizing delivery date, order quantity, price, packing and packaging details, factory name, method of freight and freight carrier.

Size set samples: Samples produced in the correct measurements for fit-testing purposes. Full (the entire size range) or broken (selected sizes in the range) size sets need to be produced to identify any fit issues prior to the start of production.

Specifications or specs come in many formats; some of the main ones are discussed next:

- Size spec: Body measurement chart needed to produce sales/counter samples, size set samples, pre-production and production garments

- Design spec: Front and back view of the garment containing stitching details, print/embroidery positioning
- Fabrication spec: Contains information on the assembly of the garment, the equipment used and the stitch types and density
- Colour and fabric spec: Stipulates the Pantone number or fabric swatch for colour reference; it contains the fabric type and its weight when applicable and the fibre content
- Testing spec: As well as the required (BSI) requirements, some specific tests might have to be carried out on the cloth or the garment.

Global sourcing: A strategy which aims to find and evaluate suitable sources of supply globally.

Master carton: The cardboard box containing the garments and marked with the order details prior to being loaded onto a freight container. Inner cartons are contained within the master carton and are also marked with the order details: they represent an added expense and should be avoided whenever possible.

7

MARGINAL COSTING

Introduction

At the beginning of Chapter 2 we noted that there are a number of ways in which costs can be classified. We also noted that one way to consider costs is based on their behaviour. If the costs of a manufacturing business are considered, it can be seen that some costs relate closely to the product being made, such as the direct materials used in the product and the direct labour used to make the product. Whereas some costs relate to the business as a whole, they are not product specific and are often based over periods of time, like rental of a factory unit, or business rates, or management salaries.

This classification of costs is used in a system of costing called *marginal costing,* and this can add to our overall understanding of costs and can provide a useful method of considering cost in the decision-making process.

Variable Costs

Those costs that relate specifically to the product being made are referred to as *variable* or *marginal costs*—they tend to increase in proportion to the output of the product being made. Thus the more garments you make, the greater the amount of fabric that will be needed, and on the whole the amount of fabric required will increase in proportion to the number of garments being produced; therefore the fabric cost will increase with the output.

However, because each garment (of the same type) uses the same amount of fabric, then the unit cost of the variable costs is the same per garment.

In manufacture of fashion garments the following would be typical variable costs:

Fabric
Thread
Trimmings
Fastenings—buttons, etc.

Interlining
Cutters' wages
Machinists' wages
Royalties
Press room wages

Fixed Costs

Those costs that relate to the business as a whole and are not specifically related to the product being made are called *fixed costs*, and as these often relate to periods of time they are also sometimes referred to as *period costs*. These costs are fixed over periods of time, like rent and business rates. That is not to say that rent and rates do not increase; indeed they usually increase from one year to the next, but they remain fixed over given periods of time and they do not increase with the output of the product.

However, this means that the fixed cost per unit cost decrease as output increases. This can be illustrated by a simple example of rent for a factory unit. A manufacturer pays £100,000 per annum in rent. If the company produces 50,000 garments in that period, then the rent is £2 per garment, but if it produces 100,000 garments, then the unit cost is £1 per garment.

In the manufacture of fashion garments the following are typical fixed costs:

Rental of a factory unit, offices, etc.
Business rates
Management salaries
Certain types of loan interest
Insurance premiums

Semi-Variable Costs

Inevitably in all businesses there are some complex costs that do not easily sit in either the variable or fixed categories; they often contain an element of both. These are known as *semi-variable costs* or *semi-fixed costs*. These costs have fixed and variable elements which can sometimes be identified, but not always.

A typical example of a semi-variable cost in clothing manufacture might be supervisors' wages and salaries, where the supervisor is paid a fixed wage for supervisory work but may also be paid additionally for garments produced on the production line.

In the manufacture of fashion garments other typical semi-variable costs would be:

Power—electricity (standing charge and a charge for electricity units consumed)
Depreciation of machinery
Maintenance

So far we have considered costs and we have made the connection, in the earlier chapters, between cost and profit—the revenue for the year minus the costs, giving the profit for the year. Marginal costs concern the profit for the business as a whole as well as the *contribution* that each product makes to the fixed costs of the business and the overall profit.

We calculate contribution by taking the revenue generated by the product and deducting the variable costs. The revenue the product(s) generate are generally referred to as the sales. Therefore the calculation of the contribution is as follows:

contribution = sales – variable costs

Example

Modus Shirts, a garment manufacturer, has three products—sweatshirts, polo shirts and T-shirts—and they sell with varying degrees of success.

Sales

sweatshirts, £140,000; polo shirts, £100,000; T-shirts, £50,000

They incur direct materials and direct labour costs that form their variable costs for each product.

Variable Costs

sweatshirts, £72,000; polo shirts, £56,000; T-shirts, £48,000

The factory also incurs rent and business rates and a range of other fixed costs that amount to £44,000 for the year.

Modus Shirts' marginal cost statement is shown in Table 7.1.

You can see in Table 7.1 that the information for Modus Shirts has been put into a marginal cost format and that the contribution for each product has been calculated. Note that the fixed costs have been deducted from the total contribution only in order to obtain the profit for the business as a whole.

The contribution shows how much each product will add or contribute to the business to meet the fixed costs of the business and increase the profits. In the Modus Shirts example you can see that each of the products makes a positive contribution; thus they all contribute something to the fixed costs of the business and the overall profitability. The objective is to increase the contribution that the products make to ensure meeting the fixed costs and increasing the profits.

TABLE 7.1 Modus Shirts marginal cost statement

	Sweatshirts £'000	Polo shirts £'000	T-shirts £'000	Total £'000
Sales	140	100	50	290
Less variable costs	72	56	48	176
Contribution	**68**	**44**	2	**114**
Fixed costs				44
Net profit				**70**

TABLE 7.2 Amended Modus Shirts marginal cost statement

	Sweatshirts £'000	Polo Shirts £'000	T-shirts £'000	Total £'000
Sales	140	100	50	290
Less variable costs	72	56	52	180
Contribution	**68**	**44**	(2)	**110**
Fixed costs				44
Net profit				**66**

Management needs to carefully consider those products that show a negative contribution, and if their position cannot be improved to give a positive contribution, then they may need to be eliminated from the range and the capacity used for something else.

Had the variable costs for producing the T-shirts in the Modus Shirts example been £52,000, then this would have produced a negative contribution for T-shirts and a very different outcome for the business, as illustrated in Table 7.2.

In this situation Modus Shirts would have to decide what to do with a product range that gives a negative contribution and therefore reduces the business's overall profit. Under certain circumstances management may be prepared to accept a negative contribution if doing so enables them to sell more of their other products, but as a rule of thumb negative contributions should be eliminated.

Before reading on, you should now consider what action Modus could take in these circumstances. These are some of the options available to Modus's management:

1. Determine whether the T-shirts could stand an increase in price to increase the sales revenue
2. Look at controlling the costs of the T-shirts to reduce the variable costs and give a positive contribution—perhaps better fabric utilisation
3. Enact steps 1 and 2 in tandem to give a positive contribution
4. Eliminate the T-shirts from the product range and see if the spare capacity could be used for a product that would give a positive contribution—perhaps making hoodies
5. Eliminate the T-shirts from the product range and use the spare capacity to make more sweatshirts and polo shirts if the market exists for the increased output
6. Do some combination of steps 4 and 5.

Treatment of the Semi-Variable Costs

As mentioned earlier, most businesses will have some costs that do not easily fit into the variable or fixed categories. They usually have an element of both in them, and the variable/fixed elements are often not easy to separate. The semi-variable costs in marginal costing are split into their respective fixed and variable elements. This can be done with varying degrees of success depending on the nature of the cost but may require some estimation.

A typical and relatively simple example would be supervisors' wages, where a supervisor is paid a fixed wage for her supervisory work but receives additional payment in proportion to work done on the production line that contributes to making garments. Thus this semi-variable cost would be simple to apportion between its fixed and variable elements.

A more complex semi-variable cost would be power or electricity, as this may have a fixed standing charge and a rate for electricity consumed, though in some circumstances there may be several rates for the units consumed. Clearly the standing charge is a fixed cost and the running of machinery will probably be the major user of the units of electricity consumed, but electricity will be used in other parts of the business—the offices, for lighting, heating and the like. Thus the power charge is not a simple divide between its fixed element and the charge for units of electricity consumed. A similar problem could well arise with maintenance. In these circumstances management will have to make decisions about the proportions of semi-variable cost to be considered fixed and variable.

Example

This example shows how the semi-variable costs might be treated in a marginal cost statement. Table 7.3 shows the costs for a small manufacturer over a coming period. The intention is to produce 10,000 standard garments in this period at a selling price of £6.50 each (£65,000).

In the marginal cost statement (Table 7.4) all the variable costs will be grouped together (under their respective products if there are several) and all the fixed costs are grouped together.

TABLE 7.3

Cost	Type of Cost	Amount of Cost	Cost at 10,000 Garment Output
Direct materials	Variable	£2.85 per garment	£28,500
Direct labour	Variable	£2 per garment	£20,000
Rent/Business rates	Fixed	£4,000 for the period	£5,000
Supervision	Semi-variable	£4,000 fixed plus £0.25 per garment	Fixed £6,000 Var £2,500
Heat/Light/Power	Semi-variable	£500 fixed plus £0.5 per garment	Fixed £500 Var £5,000

TABLE 7.4 Marginal cost statement

	£
Sales (10,000 × £6.50)	65,000
Less variable costs (£5.60* × 10,000)	56,000
Contribution	9,000
Fixed costs (£4,000 + £4,000 + £500)	8,500
Net profit	500

The variable costs are made up of the direct materials, the direct labour and the variable elements of the supervision and the heat, light and power.

£2.85 + £2.00 + £0.25 + £0.50 = £5.60

Case Study

Country Style is a somewhat conservative business, making men's hacking-style jackets and gilets. The company has analyzed its cost and anticipated sales for the next half year and has come up with the figures as reported in Table 7.5.

The fixed costs for the period have been calculated at £150,000.

TABLE 7.5

Jacket Styles	The Dale	The Glen	The Gilet
Selling price to retailers	£28.50	£40.00	£25.00
Variable costs per style	£25.50	£37.00	£21.50
Estimated sales (based on orders in garments)	24,000	13,500	10,000

TABLE 7.6 Marginal cost statement existing business

	The Dale £	The Glen £	The Gilet £	Total £
Sales	684,000	540,000	250,000	1,474,000
Less variable costs	612,000	499,500	215,000	1,326,500
Contribution	72,000	40,500	35,000	147,500
Fixed costs				150,000
Net profit (Loss)				(2,500)

Given that business has contracted in recent years, the factory does have some spare capacity and additional business would be welcome. They have another potential order for the period for a significant number of jackets, but it would require producing the Glen style with some modifications to suit an overseas buyer, and this would increase the variable costs of these jackets by £0.50. The order is potentially for 5,000 in the period and may lead to further work. However, in addition to the increase in the variable costs for these special Glen jackets, the customer wants a reduced price and is prepared to pay only £38.00 per jacket.

Issues Raised

1. Management need to consider their current position given the business they have.
2. Management need to consider the impact of the new order and whether increased costs and a lower selling price are viable—assuming that they have the capacity for the order (see Table 7.6).

TABLE 7.7 Marginal cost statement existing plus potential business

	The Dale £	The Glen £	The Glen Modified £	The Gilet £	Total £
Sales	684,000	540,000	190,000	250,000	1,664,000
Less variable costs	612,000	499,500	187,500	215,000	1,514,000
Contribution	72,000	40,500	2,500	35,000	150,000
Fixed costs					150,000
Net Profit					—

You can see that on the basis of the existing business they would show a small loss for the period, though, notably, all the product lines show a positive contribution.

The figures for Table 7.7 are calculated by multiplying the sales and variable costs figures given in the case study by the number of estimated number of garment to be sold. Thus sales for the Dale are £28.50 × 24,000 = £684,000 (see Table 7.7).

The figures for the modified Glen are calculated by taking the original Glen figures and adjusting them to take account of the revised data relating to the potential order. Thus the selling price becomes £38.00 per garment and the variable cost £37.50 per garment. The contribution on the potential business is very slim—only £0.50 per garment—but it can be seen (Table 7.7) that this would be enough to enable the business to break even (i.e. make no profit and no loss) in the coming period. The company hopes that if fulfilled satisfactorily, it will lead to more overseas business with bigger contributions.

Exercises and Activities

1. Fixed/Variable/Semi-Variable

For the list of costs given in Exercise Table 7.1, indicate whether they are likely to be fixed, variable or semi-variable costs for a clothing manufacturer.

2. Fallowfield Fashions

From the data for Fallowfield Fashions shown in Exercise Table 7.2, prepare a marginal cost statement clearly showing the contribution made by each product. The fixed overheads for the period are estimated to be £140,000.

EXERCISE TABLE 7.1

Cost	Fixed	Variable	Semi-variable
Thread			
Building insurance premiums			
Heat, light & power			
Interlining			
Shirt buttons			
Factory manager's salary			
Fusing press operators' wages			
Business rates			
Stationery			
Telephone			
Cutting room wages			
Receptionists' wages			
Press room wages			
Zips for trousers			
Boxes for a boxed shirt			
Delivery vehicle costs			
Canteen staff wages			
Bank loan interest			
Bank charges			
Fabric for dresses			

EXERCISE TABLE 7.2

	Shirts (Long-sleeved) £'000	Shirts (Short-sleeved) £'000	Blouses, Style A £'000	Blouses, Style B £'000
Direct materials (variable)	90	72	60	60
Direct labour (variable)	50	40	30	40
Variable overheads	5	3	2	3
Sales	200	160	90	150

EXERCISE TABLE 7.3

	Style A	Style B	Style C
Direct materials cost	£16,800	£13,000	£11,680
Direct labour costs	£7,700	£7,000	£7,840
Variable overheads	£2,100	£2,400	£2,080
Sales in garments (orders)	700	1,000	800
Selling price	£50	£32	£34

The management of Fallowfield Fashions have considered dropping the Blouse Style A product. Suggest what effect taking this action would have on the business.

3. Melton Fashions

Melton Fashion makes ladies' dresses and for the coming four-week period have three styles in production. Exercise Table 7.3 shows the costs for the period and the orders received. The fixed costs for the period are estimated at £20,000.

They have received an enquiry about a further order for 500 Style C dresses, but the customer wants the price reduced to £31.

Prepare a marginal cost statement for the confirmed business for the period.

Prepare a revised marginal cost statement to include the new order at the reduced price, assuming that the business has the capacity to meet this order.

Comment on whether the new business should be accepted and why or why not.

Further Reading

Drury, C. (2003), *Cost and Management Accounting: An Introduction* (5th edn), London: Thomson Learning.

Drury, C. (2005), *Management Accounting for Business* (3rd edn), London: Thomson Learning.

Drury, C. (2008), *Management and Cost Accounting* (7th edn), London: Thomson Learning.

Horngren, C. T., Sundem, G. L., and Stratton, W. O. (2008), *Introduction to Management Accounting* (14th edn), Harlow: Pearson Prentice Hall.

Lucey, T. (2009), *Costing* (7th edn), London: Cengage Learning.

Russell, D., Patel, A., and Wilkinson-Riddle, G. (2002), *Cost Accounting an Essential Guide,* Harlow: Prentice Hall.

8

BREAK-EVEN ANALYSIS

Introduction

This chapter on break-even analysis uses the same classification of costs as the previous chapter on marginal costing. Indeed it is an extension of marginal costing as well as the use of fixed and variable cost thinking. The objective of break-even analysis is to establish the point at which the business will reach its break-even point. The break-even point is the point at which the business will make neither a profit nor a loss; the revenues will exactly cover the costs.

In the short term this is a useful piece of information as it gives management an understanding of what level of business they need to achieve to at least cover their costs. Beyond the break-even point the business will go into profit. Thus the sooner the business passes through its break-even point, the sooner it will earn a profit.

Establishing the Break-Even Point

There are a number of ways in which the break-even point can be established:

1. By tabulating the output, costs and revenues of the business and seeing where the break-even point falls in the table
2. By constructing a break-even chart and graphically establishing where the break-even point falls, or a variation on this, such as a profit/volume chart
3. By calculating the break-even point

Break-Even Tabulation

The break-even tabulation essentially matches the fixed costs and the variable costs at different levels of output with the revenues generated at those levels of output.

Example

Morning Breaks Ltd have received an order to make 5,000 dresses. The customer is prepared to pay £15 for each dress, making the total order worth £75,000.

The fixed costs for the period are as follows:

Rent	£9,000
Business rates	1,200
Loan interest	250
Insurance	300
Other fixed costs	1,250
Total	£12,000

The variable costs of making the dresses are as follows:

Direct materials	£6.00
Direct labour	3.00
Power	2.00
Other variable costs	1.00
Per dress	£12.00

The data for Morning Breaks Ltd can now be analysed in a table, taking the cost data to different levels of output activity, up to completion of the 5,000 dresses. The table starts at zero dresses produced and goes to 5,000 in increments of 1,000 (see Table 8.1).

The fixed costs are for the whole period, so they are not affected by the level of output; thus the fixed cost column is the same (£12,000) at whatever level of output. The variable costs increase with output; thus it is the output multiplied by the variable cost per dress.

TABLE 8.1

No. of Garments Produced	Fixed Costs (for period) £	Variable Costs (per dress) £	Total Costs (FC + VC) £	Value of Sales £	Profit or (loss) £
0	12,000	0	12,000	0	(12,000)
1,000	12,000	12,000	24,000	15,000	(9,000)
2,000	12,000	24,000	36,000	30,000	(6,000)
3,000	12,000	36,000	48,000	45,000	(3,000)
4,000	12,000	48,000	60,000	60,000	BEP
5,000	12,000	60,000	72,000	75,000	3,000

The sales value increases with output, so it is the output multiplied by the selling price per dress.

At 4,000 dresses produced, the total costs (£60,000) and the value of the sales (£60,000) are the same—the revenues cover the costs. This is the break-even point (BEP).

Beyond this point the business goes into a profit situation, and you can see that on the completed order of 5,000 dresses a modest profit of £3,000 is achieved.

A tabulation will not always show exactly where the break-even point falls, but it will give a close indication.

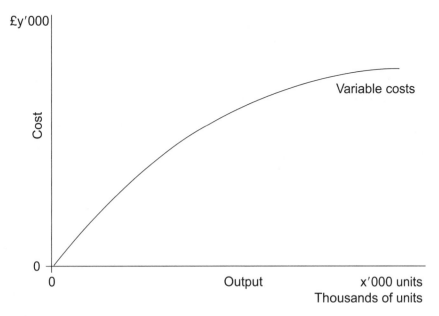

Figure 8.1   Theoretical shape of variable costs.

Break-Even Chart

The break-even chart is a graphical method of determining the break-even point. It is based on the behaviour of the fixed and variable costs.

In theory, the variable costs, if plotted on a graph, would give a gently rising curve that may fall off at the limits of output, as in Figure 8.1, and the fixed costs a straight line indicating that the fixed costs are the same at zero output as they are at x'000 garments produced, as in Figure 8.2. Accountants have a model of these which show the variable costs plotted as an ascending line (see Figure 8.3.)

Thus the break-even chart for Morning Breaks Ltd would be as shown in Figure 8.4. The break-even point can be read off at 4,000 garments produced or £60,000 in sales.

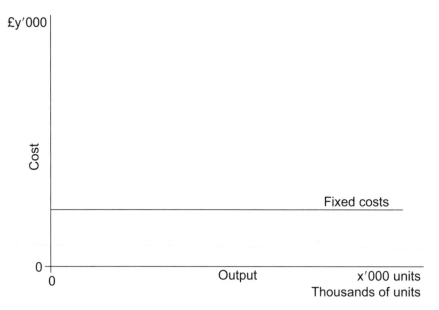

Figure 8.2 Fixed costs.

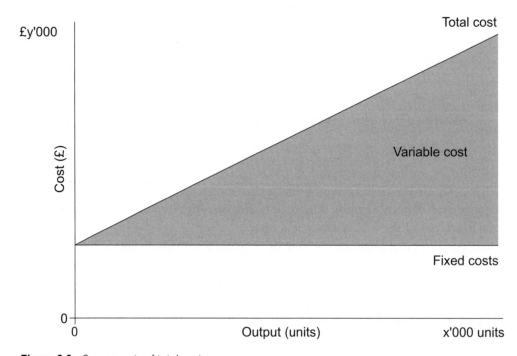

Figure 8.3 Components of total cost.

Margin of Safety

Additionally, the break-even chart also shows the margin of safety in the business (see Figure 8.4)—this is the difference between the break-even point and the target level of activity. In this case the margin of safety is 1,000 garments or £15,000 of sales. The greater the margin of safety the better, as this indicates a longer period of profitability once the business has broken even before reaching the target level of activity and will enable the business to survive better in times of recession. Thus businesses that break even quickly will have long margins of safety and stand a better chance of remaining profitable even in more difficult times. However, certainly in UK garment manufacturing, the margins of safety are often short; thus such businesses are vulnerable in more difficult times.

The margin of safety (MoS) can be calculated as:

$$profit \div (contribution/sales)$$

In the case of Morning Breaks Ltd:

$$MoS = £3,000 \div (£15,000/£75,000) = £15,000$$

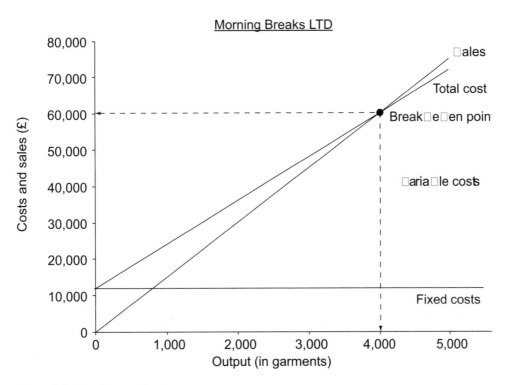

Figure 8.4   Break-even chart.

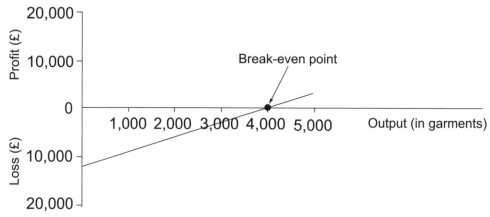

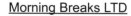

Figure 8.5 Profit/volume chart.

Profit/Volume Chart

A variation on the break-even chart is the profit/volume chart, which plots profit against output and shows the break-even point in respect of output activity; see Figure 8.5. Both the break-even chart and the profit/volume chart are useful in presentations to management when discussing break-even situations.

Break-Even Point by Calculation

The break-even point can also be calculated, though this method does not give any additional information; both the tabulation and the break-even charts are useful in terms of the other information that they provide relating to the costs of the business.

The following formula will give a calculation of the following:

$$BEP \text{ (of sales)} = FC \div \text{(contribution/sales)}$$

You will recall from Chapter 7 that contribution is sales *minus* variable costs. This formula will work at any level of sales or variable costs, but for simplicity, use the sales figure and variable costs figure at one garment, i.e. the selling price per garment and the variable costs per garment.

The Morning Breaks Ltd example would be as follows:

$$BEP = £12,000 \div [(15 - 12)/15]$$
$$BEP = £12,000 \div (3/15)$$

$$BEP = £12,000/0.2$$
$$BEP = £60,000 \text{ (Sales)}$$

or

$$BEP = £12,000 \div [(15 - 12)/15]$$
$$BEP = £12,000 \div (3/15)$$
$$BEP = £12,000 \div (1/5), \text{ then invert and multiply}$$
$$BEP = £12,000 \times 5$$
$$BEP = £60,000$$

If you want the break-even point in output, then divide by the selling price:

$$BEP \text{ of sales/selling price} = BEP \text{ in output}$$

The Morning Breaks Ltd example would be as follows:

$$£60,000/£15 = 4,000 \text{ garments}$$

Break-Even Illustration

Isolo Shirt Co can produce 20,000 men's shirts per week in a range of colours and standard sizes and have a market for that kind of output—over a forty-eight-week year this amounts to an annual output of 960,000 shirts. The selling price of their shirt varies a little with discounting but is based on an average of £3 per shirt.

The variable costs also vary slightly with colour and size but on average are as shown in Table 8.2. The fixed costs for the factory are budgeted at £250,000 per annum. Over the whole forty-eight-week year, the picture would be as shown in Table 8.3. The margin of safety would be as follows:

$$MoS = £230,000 \div (£0.5/£3.00) = £1,380,000$$

TABLE 8.2

Direct materials	£1.50
Direct labour	£0.40
Variable overheads	£0.60
Total per shirt	£2.50

TABLE 8.3

Output in shirts	Fixed costs £	Variable costs £	Total costs £	Value of sales £	Profit (Loss) £
0	250,000	0	250,000	0	(250,000)
20,000	250,000	50,000	300,000	60,000	(240,000)
100,000	250,000	250,000	500,000	300,000	(200,000)
200,000	250,000	500,000	750,000	600,000	(150,000)
400,000	250,000	1,000,000	1,250,000	1,200,000	(50,000)
500,000	250,000	1,250,000	1,500,000	1,500,000	BEP
750,000	250,000	1,875,000	2,125,000	2,250,000	125,000
800,000	250,000	2,000,000	2,250,000	2,400,000	150,000
960,000	250,000	2,400,000	2,650,000	2,880,000	230,000

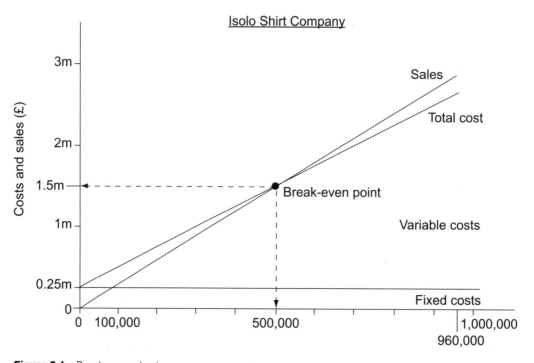

Figure 8.6   Break-even chart.

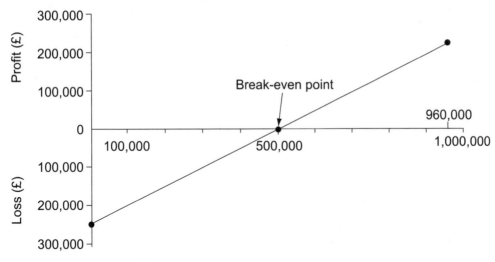

Figure 8.7 Profit/volume chart.

Using the data from the table the break-even chart and the profit-volume chart would look like Figures 8.6 and 8.7.

Exercises and Activities

1. Your Event Ltd have the following fixed and variable costs in a period when they hope to make between 6,000 and 7,000 garments. Their average selling price is £56 per garment.

    Using the fixed costs shown in Exercise Table 8.1 and the variable costs shown in Exercise Table 8.2, do the following:

EXERCISE TABLE 8.1

Rent	£18,000
Business rates	£8,800
Loan interest	£4,000
Other fixed overheads	£1,200
Total	**£32,000**

EXERCISE TABLE 8.2

Direct materials	£25
Direct labour	13
Variable overheads	10
Total	**£48**

Construct a table showing the output from 0 to 7,000 garments in 1,000-garment increments.
Construct a break-even chart.
Calculate the break-even point.

2. Using the data from Your Event Ltd (Exercise 1), construct a profit/volume chart.
3. A business making and selling specialist riding jackets incurs fixed costs of £70,000 for a period and a variable cost per jacket of £24. Their selling price falls between £30 and £36 per jacket depending on the customer.

   Consider the situation where one large customer pays £25 per jacket and all others pay £32 per jacket. The large customer represents 75 per cent of the sales in the period.
   What would the level of sales have to be to break even in the period?
   Construct a profit/volume chart for the business showing it going into profit for the period.

4. A bootmaker is seeking to sell 14,000 pairs of boots in a period. The boots have a variable cost of £15 per pair to make, and the fixed costs for the period are £47,000 with a required profit of £23,000.

   At what figure should the bootmaker set the selling price?
   At this selling price, at what point will the bootmaker break even?

Further Reading

Drury, C. (2003), *Cost and Management Accounting: An Introduction* (5th edn), London: Thomson Learning.
Drury, C. (2005), *Management Accounting for Business Decisions* (3rd edn), London: Thomson Learning.
Drury, C. (2008), *Management and Cost Accounting* (7th edn), London: Thomson Learning.
Horngren, C. T., Sundem, G. L., and Stratton, W. O. (2008), *Introduction to Management Accounting* (14th edn), Harlow: Pearson Prentice Hall.
Lucey, T. (2009), *Costing* (7th edn), London: Cengage Learning.
Russell, D., Patel, A., and Wilkinson-Riddle, G. (2002), *Cost Accounting: An Essential Guide,* Harlow: Prentice Hall.

9

BUDGETING AND STANDARD COSTING

Introduction

This chapter provides an introduction to standard costing and budgeting. The topics are closely related to each other in that budgeting is a planning process intent on producing a financial plan for the business for a future period. Standard costing is a system of costing based upon using predetermined costs.

There can be standard costs for direct materials, direct labour and fixed and variable overheads. It is then customary to use the standard costs in the costing process and compare the standard costs to the actual costs incurred; the difference is known as the *variance*. This process of comparison, standard cost to actual cost, is referred to as *variance analysis*. In businesses where standard costing is used, it forms an important part of the cost management of the business.

Budgeting

A budget is a financial plan for a future period and budgeting is the process of achieving that plan. Note that the budget is a plan—not just an estimate or a forecast, but a plan of action. It is expressed in financial terms, i.e. money with targets for sales, and production converted into money. It is for a future period, normally the coming year, though businesses may have longer-term plans, particularly for capital expenditure.

All businesses should produce budgets and have plans as to where the business is going. Often small businesses do not plan well, and sometimes when they are forced to plan—as, say, when they apply for a bank loan—even though they have produced a plan, they do very little with it. Bigger businesses are better at planning and better at budgeting. Students going into the employ of larger organizations will almost certainly have to work to the budgetary requirements of that business.

The budget needs to be integrated across the business; separate departments cannot produce their budgets in isolation, because one element of the business impacts on another. Thus the sales budget needs to fit with the production budget. This will be key to determining the amounts of direct materials required and the budgeted costs of direct labour.

Crucial to the whole operation of the business will be the cash budget—the plan of the business's cash flow. Essentially this shows the anticipated cash coming into the business month by month and the scheduled expenditure month by month. Thus the balances of cash at the end of each period can be seen, and the need for additional funding or overdraft facilities can be anticipated.

The Cash Budget

The cash budget is usually organized on a monthly basis as shown in Table 9.1 and summarizes the budgeted receipts and budgeted payments. At the end of the month the balance (positive or negative) is calculated and carried forward to the next month.

TABLE 9.1

	April £	May £	June £	July £	August £	Sept £
Budgeted receipts						
Sales (debtors)						
Loans						
Total budgeted receipts						
Budgeted payments						
Creditors						
Wages & salaries						
Business rates						
Utilities						
Capital expenditure						
Loan repayments						
Taxes						
Total budgeted payments						
Net cash*						
Balance brought forward						
Balance carried forward						

The net cash* designation is the difference between the budgeted receipts and the budgeted payments. This means that on a month-by-month basis it can be seen whether the business's receipts are covering the budgeted payments.

Example of a Cash Budget

Osborne Trading Ltd has the following budgeted receipts and payments for the coming six-month period. At the beginning of January they have £960 cash in the bank. The figures have been simplified to illustrate the principle (see Table 9.2).

TABLE 9.2

	Jan £	Feb £	Mar £	Apr £	May £	Jun £
Receipts from customers	1,800	1,800	2,500	3,600	3,800	4,200
Creditors	600	1,000	1,000	1,400	1,200	1,200
Rent & rates	1,200	1,200	1,200	1,600	1,200	1,200
Wages	500	500	500	500	500	500
Electricity			300			280
Insurances				200		
Sundries	50	50	50	50	50	50

Osborne Trading Ltd Cash Budget Statement

The budgeted receipts in this case are not total in that there is only one figure in each month— the budgeted sales income (see Table 9.3). The budgeted payments are totalled and deducted from the budgeted receipts to give the net cash figure. If the budgeted payments are greater than the budgeted receipts this will be a negative figure and is shown in brackets.

For January: £1,800 – £2,350 = £(550) net cash

The balance of cash from the previous month (the balance brought forward) is then added to the net cash to give the closing balance for the month.

For January: £(550) + £960 = £410 balance carried forward.

The balance carried forward at the end of the month then goes into the next month as the balance brought forward.

TABLE 9.3

	Jan £	Feb £	Mar £	Apr £	May £	Jun £
Budgeted receipts						
Sales	1,800	1,800	2,500	3,600	3,800	4,200
Budgeted payments						
Creditors	600	1,000	1,000	1,400	1,200	1,200
Rent & rates	1,200	1,200	1,200	1,600	1,200	1,200
Wages	500	500	500	500	500	500
Electricity			300			280
Insurances				200		
Sundries	50	50	50	50	50	50
Total budgeted payments	2,350	2,750	3,050	3,750	2,950	3,230
Net cash	(550)	(950)	(550)	(150)	850	970
Balance brought forward	960	410	(540)	(1,090)	(1,240)	(390)
Balance carried forward	410	(540)	(1,090)	(1,240)	(390)	580

Sales Lag

When the business has prepared its sales budget, the budgeted income from this cannot just be put into the cash budget. The cash budget is a plan of receipts and payments, and it is unlikely that sales made in one month will result in their income being received in that month. Most businesses operate on trade credit so from the time when sales are made the income will not be received for one, two or even up to three months. This is known as the sales lag. The sales budget needs to be converted into a plan showing when the income will be received. The easiest way of doing this is to use *sales lag analysis.*

Example

Table 9.4 shows, down the left-hand column, the sales budget for the coming period. The analysis columns going across the page from left to right show when the budgeted sales will be received by the business, assuming that the normal trade credit rules are followed. In this situation the business operates on two months' trade credit being extended. The figures on the bottom line of Table 9.4 will go into the cash budget as the budgeted receipts.

TABLE 9.4   Sales Lag Analysis

Budgeted sales	Jan £	Feb £	Mar £	Apr £	May £	Jun £	Jul £	Aug £
Jan £4,500			4,500					
Feb £5,000				5,000				
Mar £5,200					5,200			
Apr £5,600						5,600		
May £5,800							5,800	
Jun £6,800								6,800
Jul £6,800								
Budgeted receipts			**4,500**	**5,000**	**5,200**	**5,600**	**5,800**	**6,800**

Flexible Budgets

Flexible budgeting is a system of budgeting sometimes used in manufacturing where a series of budgets are produced dependent on different levels of output activity. It uses the fixed and variable behaviour of costs outlined in Chapter 7 and recognizes that some costs remain fixed for periods of time whilst others increase with output. A flexible budget enables management to see the effect of over- or undershooting the output targets and the associated costs.

Example

A clothing manufacturer has the following budgeted costs:

Direct materials: £3.00 per garment (variable)
Direct labour: £1.20 per garment (variable)
Fixed overheads: £20,000 for the period (fixed)

The target in the period is 25,000 garments (see Table 9.5). For the variable costs the budgeted cost per unit is multiplied by the level of output—direct materials £3.00 × 25,000, and so forth. The fixed costs remain fixed for the period and are not affected by the level of output. The process of examining the costs at different levels of output is known as *flexing the budget*.

TABLE 9.5   Flexible Budget

	Output 23,000 £	Output 24,000 £	Target Output 25,000 £	Output 26,000 £
Direct materials cost	69,000	72,000	75,000	78,000
Direct labour cost	27,600	28,800	30,000	31,200
Fixed overhead	20,000	20,000	20,000	20,000
Total budget	116,600	120,800	125,000	129,200
Budgeted unit cost	5.07	5.03	5.00	4.97

In this type of budgetary exercise the issue of semi-variable costs often arises—as mentioned previously, a semi-variable cost is one that has within it a fixed and a variable element. In such circumstances management have to have decided how they will disaggregate the elements of such costs.

Example

Supervision might be seen to be a semi-variable cost with the fixed element being £15,000 over the period with £0.25 per unit of output. Thus the cost in a flexible budget similar to that depicted in Table 9.5 would look like that shown in Table 9.6.

TABLE 9.6

	23,000	24,000	25,000	26,000
Supervision £15,000 + £0.25 per unit	£20,750	£21,000	£21,250	£21,500

Zero-Based Budgeting

The traditional way of preparing budgets was on an incremental basis, or taking the existing budget and adjusting it for the coming year. This would take account of inflation (deflation), new activities and declining activities but would essentially be a revised version of the existing budget.

Though still widely adopted, this methodology suffers in that the business does not take a real look at its activities and tends to perpetuate the budget classifications it has always used. With changing patterns of business this may become inappropriate and make the budget less of a strategic plan.

Zero-based budgeting (ZBB) has been in existence for some time and is gradually gaining in recognition. Essentially, in ZBB each budget category has an expenditure level of zero until the responsible budget holder makes a case for the budget and justifies the activity that causes the cost. Thus in ZBB the activities are re-evaluated each year when the budget is created, providing a very proactive approach to budgeting.

In theory ZBB should result in a better allocation of resources and should focus attention on value for money. In practice it may be time-consuming and may require better training in order for staff to operate the system. As a system it is widely used in the USA and is used by many businesses, public authorities and non-profit-making organizations in the UK and Europe.

Standard Costing

A *standard cost* is a predetermined cost for an activity required to make a product. It is normally expressed on a unit basis. Thus in garment manufacture there might be a standard cost for direct materials in a particular garment and similarly for direct labour and overhead costs.

In setting the standard costs, the business will take into account current costs for materials, labour and the like and may take into account reasonable estimates for changes in the economic environment such as inflation (or deflation) or pay awards pending and try to achieve a realistic attainable cost. When the standard costs are compared to the actual costs, any difference (variance) is significant and may have come about through working practices, and if it is more than a few per cent it may require investigation. Some textbooks suggest that a system of standard costing brings about a synergy between the management accounting function and production managers because to achieve realistic standard costs, the two factions must work together. Certainly standard costing does require different parts of the business to cooperate in achieving the standard costs. Standard costs do need to be periodically reviewed, and this should be done at least annually.

Standard costing tends to lend itself to larger manufacturing organizations that make a fairly uniform product involving similar amounts of direct materials and direct labour with uniform processes. A shirt factory or a nightwear factory might be examples where it could be used in clothing manufacture. It would probably not be suitable for a factory making, say, men's suits with relatively short runs and big variations in styles and fabrics.

Variance Analysis

Variance analysis is the comparison of the standard costs with the actual costs incurred. Any differences in this comparison process are known as *variances*. Clearly variances may be to the advantage or disadvantage of the business—i.e. costing less than standard or more than standard.

More than Standard

Adverse variances occur where the actual costs incurred are greater than the standard cost set. The cost to the business is greater than the planned or predetermined costs, and this means that the business is moving adversely away from its targets.

Less than Standard

Favourable variances occur where the actual costs incurred are less than the predetermined standard cost set. The cost to the business is less than the planned or predetermined costs, and this means that the business has made savings on its targets set.

The usefulness of the variances to management in controlling costs relies on realistic, attainable standards being set. So the variance analysis will be as only good as the standards. Poor or loosely set standards will give variances that are of little use.

Both the adverse and favourable variances should be reported to management. Management may need to act upon adverse variances to correct matters that are going wrong and steer the business back to its planned costs. If savings have been made, management may also want to try to see if these have come about through improved practices that could be more widely used. However, favourable variances in one area of the business, and therefore cost savings there, might throw up adverse variances in another area. Management will want to make careful scrutiny of all variances, adverse or favourable, in order to better manage the costs of the business.

Example

A factory's fabric buyer purchases a quantity of fabric from a supplier and is able to get it at a reduced price. Consequently his variance in terms of price is favourable—seemingly a saving having been made.

However, the production manager finds that he has to use more of the fabric in production than is normally required because the cheaper fabric has rather more faults in it than usual. The variance in terms of the amount used is therefore adverse, giving an overspending on fabric used in the production department.

Management have to decide what variances (adverse and favourable) are significant, because with this type of costing system there will nearly always be some variance. Figure 9.1 illustrates a system that management might adopt, though the percentages shown here are just a guide. Different businesses may have different views on this.

You can seen from Figure 9.1 that there is a band of variances between −5% and +5% where no action is taken. However, above or below this band, action is required, as these would be significant variances. Different businesses may operate to different levels of tolerance, and the percentage figures shown here are just to illustrate the principle.

Above 10%—requires urgent attention
+5% to +10%—requires investigation; the costing should be better than this.
0% to 5%—no action required
0%
0% to –5%—no action required
–5% to –10%—requires investigation; the costing should be better than this.
Below –10%—requires urgent attention

Figure 9.1

Direct Materials

For the elements of cost there will be a net variance that can be split into its respective parts—price variance and usage variance. If, for example, in the case of direct materials relating to a garment, there will be a variance between the standard cost and the actual cost, this can then be further analysed to see how much of the variance relates to differences in the price paid for the materials and how much relates to the amount of the materials used to produce the garment.

Example

Job No: AB123

Direct materials

Standard cost: 120 metres fabric @ £3.50 per metre
Actual cost: 125 metres @ £3.45 per metre (see Table 9.7)

TABLE 9.7

Standard cost	120 × £3.50	£420.00
Actual cost	125 × £3.45	£431.25
Variance		(£11.25) Adverse

In this example the £11.25 adverse variance is caused by two factors:

1. The price paid for the fabric is lower (£3.45 against £3.50)
2. The amount of fabric used is higher (120 metres against 125 metres).

Materials price variance

Actual usage (standard price − actual price) = materials price variance
125 × (3.50 − 3.45) = £6.25 favourable (paid less for the material than expected)

Materials usage variance

Standard price (standard usage − actual usage) = materials usage variance
3.50 × (120 − 125) = £(17.50) adverse (used more than expected; see Table 9.8)

TABLE 9.8

Materials price variance	£6.25 Favorable
Materials usage variance	£(17.50) Adverse
Net variance	£(11.25) Adverse

In this example the net variance of £11.25 adverse represents 4 per cent of the standard cost (£11.25/£420 × 100) and therefore may not be considered to be that significant.

Example

Job No: AB124

Direct materials

Standard cost: 120 metres fabric @ £3.50 per metre
Actual cost: 125 metres @ £3.60 per metre (see Table 9.9)

TABLE 9.9

Materials price variance	125 × (£3.50 − £3.60)	£(12.50) Adverse
Materials usage variance	£3.50 × (120 − 125)	£(17.50) Adverse
Net variance	£420 (Std) − £450 (Act)	£(30.00) Adverse

In the second example both the price and the usage variances are adverse, reflecting that the business has paid more for the fabric and used more of it than planned. In this example the variance is much more significant at 7.14 per cent (£30.00/£420 × 100) and probably worthy of investigation.

Causes of Direct Materials Variances

Materials Price Variance—Favourable

Where the actual price of the direct materials is less than the standard price set, the materials price variance is said to be favourable.

1. Bulk-buying discounts or cash discounts were obtained but not considered in setting the standards.
2. Favourable exchange rates were in effect, where sourcing overseas produced a saving on the original standard price set.
3. A glut of the material has caused the price to come down.
4. The textile industry has been hit by recession and reduces its prices.
5. Cheaper, perhaps substandard, materials were purchased.

Materials Price Variance—Adverse

Where the actual price of the direct materials is greater than the standard price set, then the materials price variance is said to be adverse.

1. Inflation has pushed up the price, and this was not taken into account in setting the standards.
2. Unfavourable exchange rates have cause the real cost of the materials to be increased.
3. The price has risen owing to a shortage of the materials.
4. The material purchased is more expensive because a higher specification than required has been bought.

Materials Usage Variance—Favourable

Where the actual direct materials used is less than the standard amount set, then the materials usage variance is said to be favourable.

1. Good marker making and lay planning has given better utilization of the material.
2. There were fewer rejects in the factory than anticipated.
3. The materials purchased were of a slightly higher specification, giving less wastage.

Materials Usage Variance—Adverse

Where the actual direct materials used is greater than the standard amount set, then the materials usage variance is said to be adverse.

1. Poor lay planning led to poor utilization of the material.
2. Poor cutting required more material than planned.

3. There were more rejects in the factory than anticipated.
4. Cheap or substandard material proved difficult to work with in the factory.

Direct Labour

As with direct materials, variances can also be calculated for direct labour. The net variance can be split into two subvariances—one relating to the rate of pay and the other to the amount of direct labour used. The variance that relates to rates of pay is referred to as the *wage rate variance* and the variance that relates to the usage of direct labour is the *labour efficiency variance.*

Example

Job No: AB123

Direct labour

Standard cost: 50 hours @ £6.20 per hour
Actual cost: 52 hours @ £6.40 per hour (see Table 9.10)

TABLE 9.10

Standard cost	50 × £6.20	£310.00
Actual cost	52 × £6.40	£332.80
Variance		£(22.80) Adverse

The variance in total is adverse—the actual cost is greater than the standard cost. This is caused by both the rate per hour and the hours required being higher. We can break this variance down into its respective wage rate and efficiency variances.

Wage rate variance

Actual hours × (standard rate − actual rate) = wage rate variance
52 × (6.20 − 6.40) = £(10.40) adverse

Labour efficiency variance

Standard rate (standard hours − actual hours) = labour efficiency variance
6.20 × (50 − 52) = £(12.40) adverse (see Table 9.11)

TABLE 9.11

Wage rate variance	£(10.40) Adverse
Labour efficiency variance	£(12.40) Adverse
Net variance	£(22.80) Adverse

In total this represents a variance of 7.35% adverse (£22.80/£310.00 × 100) and therefore is significant and probably worthy of further investigation.

A further consideration with direct labour is that idle time occasionally may occur. Idle time occurs when the labour force are unable to get on with the job because of some factor that prevents their working—e.g. there is a power cut or a machine breakdown or materials have not arrived. In such cases the idle hours will be part of the actual hours, but they need to be identified separately and an idle time variance calculated so that management can see the cost of the lost production. Idle time variances are always adverse; they are lost or minus hours.

Idle time variance

$$\text{Standard rate} \times \text{idle hours} = \text{idle time variance (always adverse)}$$

Example

Job No: AB124

Direct labour

Standard cost: 50 hours @ £6.20 per hour
Actual cost: 55 hours @ £6.40 per hour

However, included in the actual hours are three hours of idle time, i.e. minus hours wherein no production could take place (see Table 9.12).

TABLE 9.12

Standard cost	50 × £6.20	£310.00
Actual cost	55 × £6.40	£352.00
Variance		£(42.00) Adverse

Wage rate variance

$$\text{Actual hours} \times (\text{standard rate} - \text{actual rate}) = \text{wage rate variance}$$
$$55 \times (6.20 - 6.40) = £(11.00) \text{ adverse}$$

Labour efficiency variance

$$\text{Standard rate} \times (\text{standard hours} - \text{actual [working] hours}) = \text{labour efficiency variance}$$
$$6.20 \times (50 - 52) = £(12.40) \text{ adverse}$$

Idle time variance

$$\text{Standard rate} \times \text{idle hours}$$
$$6.20 \times (3) = £(18.60) \text{ adverse (see Table 9.13)}$$

Note that where idle time is included in the calculation, the idle hours are not included in the actual hours for the calculation of the labour efficiency. Only the production actual hours are included.

In this example the net adverse variance is made up of an increase in the wage rate, more time being taken in production than anticipated and the loss of three hours of idle time. This would be a significant variance of 13.5 per cent (£42/£310 × 100), and management would almost certainly want to investigate it.

It may be that there is some linkage between the variances—having been forced to be idle for three hours, perhaps it was difficult for the workers to get back to full production speed, thus further extending the time the job took.

TABLE 9.13

Wage rate variance	£(11.00) Adverse
Labour efficiency variance	£(12.40) Adverse
Idle time variance	£(18.60) Adverse
Net variance	£(42.00) Adverse

Causes of Direct Labour Variances

Wage Rate Variance—Favourable

Where the wage rate paid is less than the standard wage set, then the wage rate variance is said to be favourable.

1. Pay rises were not as high as anticipated when the standards were set.
2. The job was completed without extra working in overtime as expected.
3. Less-skilled labour was used on a lower wage rate.

Wage Rate Variance—Adverse

Where the wage rate paid is greater than the standard wage set, then the wage rate variance is said to be adverse.

1. Pay rises were higher than anticipated when the standards were set.
2. Extra working in overtime required to complete the job was not anticipated.
3. More highly skilled labour was used; thus the wage rate was higher.
4. A productivity bonus was paid for doing the job in less than the standard time; this should be reflected in a saving on the labour efficiency.

Labour Efficiency Variance—Favourable

Where the time taken for the job is less than the standard time set for the job, then the labour efficiency variance is said to be favourable.

1. Productivity bonuses have reduced the time taken.
2. A better-skilled workforce have done the job in less time.

Labour Efficiency Variance—Adverse

Where the time taken for the job is greater than the standard time set for the job, then the labour efficiency variance is said to be adverse.

1. A lower-skilled workforce was used, taking more time.
2. Sickness absence affected production.
3. Technical problems arose in production.
4. Industrial action whereby the workforce have withdrawn their labour for lengths of time or deliberately reduced their productivity.

Overheads in Standard Costing

Variances can also be calculated for the overheads, but these broadly do not provide management with the same kind of control information that is apparent with the direct cost variances. It is customary to take an absorption cost approach for overheads in standard costing, similar to the approach seen in Chapter 4 but calculating a standard rate for fixed and variable overheads. The variances are then the actual overheads costs incurred against these standard rates.

Advantages and Disadvantages of Standard Costing

As with all systems, standard costing has both advantages and disadvantages. These can be summarized as follows.

Advantages

1. It provides for management by exception and gives management indicators or areas to investigate to improve performance.
2. In theory it should produce some synergy with the management accounting function and the production management team.
3. It facilitates target setting and working towards targets.
4. Once the standards are set, the process of costing should be simpler.

Disadvantages

1. It really suits only large organizations that make fairly homogeneous products.
2. It can be time-consuming in its implementation and maintenance with the setting and revision of standards.
3. Managers may not fully understand the significance of variances.

4. In situations where the business is moving into advanced manufacturing technology, it may not provide a good basis for costing; see Chapters 10 and 11.

Exercises and Activities

1. Explain what you understand by the terms *budget* and *standard cost*.
2. From the information in Exercise Table 9.1 relating to Debidall Ltd prepare a cash budget for the six months April to September. The bank balance at the beginning of April is expected to be £1,800.
3. Flare Fashions Ltd have extracted the budget information as shown in Exercise Table 9.2.
    (a) Sales are for either cash/cheque, debit or credit card. For cash/cheque and debit card sales there is no sales lag, but for credit card sales there is a one-month sales lag and the credit card company retain 8 per cent of the value of the sales. The company budgets on average for half the sales to be by credit card.
    (b) Wages and salaries are paid within the month they are incurred.
    (c) Creditors for purchases are paid in the month following purchase.

EXERCISE TABLE 9.1

	April £	May £	June £	July £	August £	Sept £
Receipts from debtors	6,400	5,400	7,400	6,800	6,300	6,500
Creditors	3,500	3,600	2,600	4,200	3,400	3,100
Wages & salaries	1,900	1,900	2,100	1,900	1,900	1,900
Heat, light & power		500			560	
Insurance				180		
Sundries	140	140	140	140	140	140

    (d) Of the overheads 35 per cent of the figure represents variable expenses, which are paid in the month after they were incurred. The remaining 65 per cent is fixed costs, of which £164,000 is depreciation. The other part of the fixed costs is paid within the month in which it is incurred.
    (e) Corporation tax of £750,000 is due in January and a dividend payment of £500,000 is payable in March.
    (f) Capital expenditure commitments of £1,000,000 and £700,000 are due in January and March, respectively.
    (g) The bank balance at 31 December is expected to be £1,450,000. You are required to:

EXERCISE TABLE 9.2

Month	Budgeted Sales £'000	Budgeted Wages & Salaries £'000	Budgeted Purchases (of stock) £'000	Budgeted Overhead £'000
October	1,200	60	335	560
November	1,100	60	405	500
December	1,000	60	365	640
January	1,400	60	335	560
February	1,200	60	370	500
March	1,100	60	360	560

     (i)   Produce a sales lag analysis as far as the data will allow.

     (ii)   Prepare a cash budget, in the net cash format, for the months January, February and March.

4.   Calculate the direct materials variances and direct labour variances from the following data:

Direct materials

Standard price per garment: £3.25
Actual price per garment: £3.30
Standard usage: 450 metres
Actual usage: 420 metres

Direct labour

Standard wage rate: £6.20 per hour
Actual wage rate: £6.25 per hour
Standard hours: 75
Actual hours: 76

5.   Collars Ltd make men's shirts of a fairly standard design in range of colours. Calculate the materials and labour variances for the following job.

Job No: DE 2367

Direct materials

Standard price: £1.25 per garment
Standard usage: 980 metres
Actual price: £1.30
Actual usage: 1,000 metres

Direct labour

Standard wage rate: £6.30 per hour
Standard hours: 3,000
Actual wage rate: £6.20 per hour
Actual hours: 3,010, including 3 hours of idle time

Further Reading

Drury, C. (2003), *Cost and Management Accounting: An Introduction* (5th edn), London: Thomson Learning.

Drury, C. (2005), *Management Accounting for Business Decisions* (3rd edn), London: Thomson Learning.

Drury, C. (2008), *Management and Cost Accounting* (7th edn), London: Thomson Learning.

Horngren, C. T., Sundem, G. L., and Stratton, W. O. (2008), *Introduction to Management Accounting* (14th edn), Harlow: Pearson Prentice Hall.

Lucey, T. (2009), *Costing* (7th edn), London: Cengage Learning.

Russell, D., Patel, A., and Wilkinson-Riddle, G. (2002), *Cost Accounting: An Essential Guide*, Harlow: Prentice Hall.

10

THE CHANGING NATURE OF COST

Introduction

Businesses and methods of manufacture and sourcing are constantly changing. High-tech methods of manufacture (known as *advanced manufacturing technology* or AMT) have been introduced into manufacturing, component manufacturing is being done in some parts of the industry and garments are being made in diverse parts of the world and shipped into their markets using an array of different logistical systems. Other systems such as *just-in-time* (JIT) and *total quality* have also been introduced. Systems and methods of production and handling are constantly being improved.

Recently in China a garment factory was making men's two-piece suits destined for a leading high street retailer in the UK. After the garments were made, they were then vacuum-packed and sent by air freight to the UK. On receipt at Stanstead Airport in the UK, they were taken to a special facility to release them from their vacuum packing and hang them conventionally for distribution across the country.

With constantly changing methods of manufacture, it would be wrong to think that methods of costing can stand still and not take account of these changes. The changing nature of the manufacturing processes and its effects on cost accounting was first identified by two American professors, Kaplan and Cooper, in the 1980s, and they began to develop costing methods to deal with the changing nature of cost.

This chapter explores the changing nature of cost and examines why the traditional methods of costing might not always be appropriate.

From Traditional to Advanced Manufacturing Technology

In traditional methods of manufacture the processes were usually driven by the direct labour. The direct labour were the skilled workforce who produced the product, and the cost of the workforce—the direct labour cost—would be a significant element of the cost. As processes become more mechanized, the costs of such mechanization increase and the direct labour costs are reduced; fewer operators are needed and skilled workers can be replaced by semi-skilled or even unskilled workers. Not all manufacturers or industries are at the same stage of development, however. Some industries are very much more high-tech than others. For example, the electronics industry, with its robot assembly, is at the sharp end of technology and will employ fewer skilled direct labour operatives than a clothing factory, where development might be hampered by the nature of fabric and cloth, which is not so easy for robots to handle.

The pathway depicted in Figure 10.1 shows on the left low-technology businesses using skilled direct labour. We are moving away from this, towards the right, where we have high-technology businesses with less use of skilled direct labour. Most businesses are somewhere in between these two extremes and will employ some technology and retain some skilled direct labour.

So as manufacturers become more mechanized and adopt more technology in their production methods, we see a reduction in the direct labour costs. The once all-important skilled workers are being replaced by fewer, semi-skilled and unskilled operators, thus reducing the direct labour costs.

At the same time the overheads of the business increase. Advanced technology does not come cheap, and it will have to be financed, often out of borrowed funds. This kind of debt needs to be serviced and will often have high interest costs associated with it. The advanced machinery itself needs attention in terms of setting up, incurring set-up costs. It will need to be cleaned and maintained, it will incur power costs and it may have to operate in a specially controlled environment. It will also depreciate. So although the direct labour costs are reduced, the overheads, and specifically the production overheads, may increase significantly.

The indirect labour costs may also increase with the use of advanced technology, as there may be greater use of machine minders and maintenance staff in place of skilled direct labour who drive the throughput of the product.

In times gone by →	Progress over time →	Now and the future
Low tech	→	High tech
High direct labour		Low direct labour
Content and cost		Content and cost

Figure 10.1   The changing nature of cost.

Just-in-Time

The move into using advanced manufacturing methods is also often linked to *just-in-time* (JIT) systems. In JIT systems it is intended that the product will be produced to the correct quality specifications at the time that it is required. Linked with this is a desire to reduce inventories (stocks of materials) so that raw materials needed in production are supplied just in time to go into production. This clearly requires some confidence that the supplier can meet the delivery date with the right materials of a suitable quality, but it does reduce inventories and the amount of capital invested in stock. It may also provide space savings, in that large storage areas for stock are no longer required and such areas can be redeployed.

These systems are also often linked to *total quality control* (TQC), where a high level of quality is sought. The emphasis in JIT is on finding out why poor quality infiltrates into production and correcting the factors that cause poor quality and rejected products. The reduction (perhaps elimination) of rejected products does in itself produce a significant cost saving and means that quality standards permeate the whole manufacturing process.

Component Manufacture and Assembly

Component manufacture and assembly has been a feature of some industries for many years. The motor car industry was probably the first industry to adopt component manufacture, in the 1950/60s. Other industries, particularly electronics, have also adopted component manufacture and assembly.

Essentially, in this system components for a product are made in different places and then sent to one plant for assembly. So in the motor car industry, the chassis is made in one place, the body shell in another, the engine block somewhere else and so on. Finally all the components are brought together in one place and assembled into a motor car.

Whilst this is not necessarily widespread in garment manufacture, it has been practiced to some extent where advance technology has been introduced. Some functions, however, still require high direct labour inputs. An example might be a lingerie manufacturer who has decided that the expensive satin and silk fabrics they use need to be carefully laid up and cut, and they have invested in a computer-driven laser-guided cutter to get that precision.

However, in terms of laying up and cutting, this piece of advanced equipment can cut and supply several sewing factories. So that is what the company do—they receive and test the fabrics at one location and cut all the component parts at that location using their high-tech cutter. The cut parts are then boxed up and sent to the sewing factories to be made up into garments. The sewing factories may be overseas in order for the company to take advantage of lower labour costs for the direct labour-driven elements of the manufacturing.

Summary of Changes in Costs with the Move into Advanced Technology

- Direct labour costs are reduced
- Production overheads are increased—power, maintenance, depreciation, environmental costs, indirect labour
- Non-production overheads are increased—interest on finance
- Inventories (stock holding) is reduced

The once-dominant direct labour cost becomes less significant compared to the increased overhead costs. Figure 10.2 illustrates this point.

This fact raises two questions:

1. Is it therefore appropriate to absorb overheads into the job costing based on direct labour costs as has been the traditional method (review Chapter 4) when the direct labour becomes a much less important element of the cost?
2. Should we be looking at what causes the overheads in order to identify their allocation to product and job costs rather than just absorbing them in an arbitrary way?

Illustration

In thinking about the two questions just raised, consider this illustration. A company produces two products, X and Y. Product X is a new product recently introduced and uses some

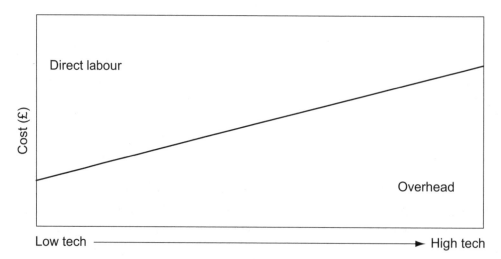

Figure 10.2 The changing nature of cost.

newly purchased advanced manufacturing equipment. This new state-of-the-art equipment produces an excellent product but at a cost—high finance charges, high set-up and maintenance costs, depreciation and cost relating to environment such as air conditioning. Product Y is more traditional and still relies on a large direct labour input.

The two products incur the same amount of direct materials costs, but product X has very little requirement for direct labour so its direct labour cost is low. Product Y, the traditionally made product, on the other hand, has high reliance on direct labour and significant direct labour costs.

The company bases its product costing on traditional absorption cost methods derived from direct labour hour cost. For each £1.00 of direct labour cost they absorb £1.50 in overhead. The direct costs for the two products X and Y are as shown in Table 10.1.

The total costs for each product based on traditional absorption costing would mean that product X would get £1.50 of overhead per unit (£1 × £1.50) and product Y would get £6.00 of overhead per unit (£4 × £1.50). This would make the total costs as shown in Table 10.2.

You can see from Figure 10.2 that the low-tech product Y gets four times the share of the overhead allocated to product X, yet it is product X, the high-tech product, that creates the high overheads in the business because of its use of advanced manufacturing technology. Product Y bears a disproportionate amount of the overhead costs and is therefore over-costed. Product X gets a small share of the overhead and is undercosted.

Thus we can see that traditional product costing methods in some cases may cause some products to be overcosted and others to be undercosted. Taken to its fullness, this may cause management to make bad acceptance or pricing decisions.

TABLE 10.1

	Product X	Product Y
Direct materials	£8.50	£8.50
Direct labour	£1.00	£4.00

TABLE 10.2

	Product X £	Product Y £
Direct materials	8.50	8.50
Direct labour	1.00	4.00
Overheads	1.50	6.00
Total cost	**11.00**	**18.50**

Cost Behaviour Change

With the move into advanced manufacturing technology and the increase in overhead cost that is associated with this move, it should be appreciated that this inevitably increases the fixed-cost element of the business. Once advanced technology equipment has been invested in, the business will have significant depreciation cost, significant finance cost and the cost of maintaining the environment for the equipment. These will be fixed costs, and these fixed overheads will have to be met from the output of the equipment. Thus a better understanding of the market, market share and new markets may be even more important where investment is made in advanced technology.

Service Industries

Traditional costing methods were rooted in manufacturing and thus gave little thought to costing in the service sector. In the latter part of the twentieth century we saw a reduction in manufacture in the UK and a rise in the service sector. In the fashion industry the extent of manufacture in the UK has dropped massively over the last twenty-five years, to be replaced by a service industry fuelled by fashion retailers sourcing fashion products from around the globe (see Chapters 5 and 6).

In these circumstances costs are important, but they do not relate to traditional systems of costing based on the elements of cost and the use of absorption costing. Thus in service industries, because that is what we are essentially talking about, different methods of treating the overheads costs are needed to ensure that management makes appropriate acceptance and pricing decisions.

Activity-Based Costing

The point has been made thus far in this chapter that changes in manufacturing and changes in the way businesses operate in some cases may mean that traditional methods of costing are inappropriate. This is particularly true where overheads have become a much more significant element of the cost. There is therefore a need for a different approach to costing. One solution put forward has been *activity-based costing* (ABC).

In ABC the activities the business engages in that create the costs are used as the drivers for driving the cost into the product with a view to giving a more balanced result in terms of product cost. The system, though developed for manufacturing, also seems to lend itself to service industries and provides them with a system of costing hitherto not available.

ABC is described, with illustration and exercises, in Chapter 11.

Exercises and Activities

1. If you are unfamiliar with some of the concepts mentioned in this chapter, such as advanced manufacturing technology and just-in-time, read around these topic areas.
2. Outline what you understand about advanced manufacturing methods and list some of the features of such methods.
3. Where a clothing business has adopted a more advanced technology approach to manufacture, explain what are likely to be the effects on their costs.

11

ACTIVITY-BASED COSTING

Introduction

This chapter considers the system of costing devised by Kaplan and Cooper to address the issues of product costing in situations where there have been changes in the nature of costs. Although this system of costing was devised for manufacturing industries, it is also applicable to service industries. Thus in fashion sourcing, where manufacture is less of a consideration and the costs relate to sourcing and transporting of the garments, *activity-based costing* may be appropriate.

It was demonstrated in Chapter 10 that as businesses change and advanced manufacturing technology comes into use, the traditional systems of product costing become less appropriate because of their reliance on direct labour cost as a driver of overheads. Once manufacturing systems change and the overheads become a much more significant element of the costs, then the business needs to look closely at the overheads and what drives them. This is also clearly the case with service businesses and those engaged solely in sourcing, given that other than the cost of the product that they buy (garments), all their other costs are effectively overheads. Thus some ways of driving those costs into the product are required, because overhead absorption based on direct labour or even machine hours is simply not an option.

Activity-Based Costing

The essence of ABC is that products or services themselves do not create cost; it is the activities that the business engages in that create cost. The product or service is a user of those activities, and the more activities a product uses, the more cost it will have to bear.

ABC tries to relate overhead to the activity that causes or drives the cost, referred to as *cost drivers*. Costs with the same cost driver are grouped together in cost pools, and an appropriate *cost driver rate* is then used to develop the product cost (see Figure 11.1). This is in contrast to traditional absorption costing, where overheads are allocated to departments

	Cost pool >	Cost driver rate >	
	Cost pool >	Cost driver rate >	
Overhead >>	Cost pool >	Cost driver rate >	**Product cost**
	Cost pool >	Cost driver rate >	
	Cost pool >	Cost driver rate >	
	Cost pool >	Cost driver rate >	

Figure 11.1 The activity-based costing process.

or cost centres where a single cost centre rate is used for all overheads in that cost centre to achieve the product costs, irrespective of what activity has caused the overhead.

Typical activities and their possible cost drivers are shown in Table 11.1.

TABLE 11.1

Typical Activity	Possible Cost Driver
Machine activity	Machine hours
Supervision	Machine hours
Set-ups	Number of set-up required
Inspection	Number of inspections
Receiving of materials	Number of receipts required

Illustration Comparing ABC to Traditional Absorption Costing

Auto Wear Overalls manufacture disposable overalls in an advanced manufacturing environment with minimal direct labour input. They produce three grades of overalls (white, green and blue) in the factory on the same equipment. The machine times for the different grades vary slightly (see Table 11.2).

TABLE 11.2

	White	Green	Blue
Planned production	100,000	80,000	60,000
Direct materials cost (per garment)	£2.00	£2.50	£3.00
Direct labour cost (per garment)	£0.35	£0.35	£0.35
Machines hours (per garment)	0.20	0.25	0.30
Number of set-ups	50	30	20

The total overheads for the period are estimated at £500,000. There are ten receipts of stock in the period, nine covering all grades and one delivery just for the white overall (see Table 11.3).

Using traditional absorption costing, absorbing the overheads based on percentage of direct labour cost, the overhead absorption rate would be 595.24 per cent.

Calculation of overhead absorption rate

White: direct labour cost £0.35 × 100,000 = £35,000
Green: direct labour cost £0.35 × 80,000 = £28,000
Blue: direct labour cost £0.35 × 60,000 = £21,000
Total direct labour cost = £84,000
£500,000/£84,000 × 100 = 595.24%

TABLE 11.3

Activity Cost Pool	Amount of Overhead	Cost Driver
Set-ups/Changeovers	£55,000	Number of set-ups
Machine activity	£150,000	Machine hours
Supervision	£200,000	
Total	£350,000	
Receiving and storage	£45,000	Number of receipts
Packing	£50,000	Output of product

Overheads absorbed by each grade of overall:

White: £35,000 × 595.24% = £208,334.00
Green:£28,000 × 595.24% = £166,667.20
Blue: £21,000 × 595.24% = £125,000.40 (see Table 11.4)

It can be seen from Table 11.4 that because the direct labour cost is uniform across the three grades, the only difference in the final unit cost is the difference in the direct materials cost—green is £0.50 more than white, and blue is £1.00 more than white. The traditional costing does not take into consideration that green and blue require more machine time per garment than white or that white will require more set-ups.

Using ABC for costing of the overheads requires more attention but gives better results, taking into account the different cost drivers of the different activities. The following example uses just four cost drivers but produces a more plausible product cost. (Some of the figures have been rounded in this example.)

Set-ups

White 50, green 30, blue 20 = 100 total
£55,000/100 = £550 per set-up
White: £550 × 50 = £27,500
Green: £550 × 30 = £16,500
Blue: £550 × 20 = £11,000

Machine activity/Supervision

White: 100,000 overalls × 0.20 = 20,000 machine hours
Green: 80,000 overalls × 0.25 = 20,000 machine hours
Blue: 60,000 overalls × 0.30 = 18,000 machine hours
Total machine hours = 58,000

TABLE 11.4 Traditional Costing—Using Percentage of Direct Labour Cost

	White £	Green £	Blue £
Direct materials	200,000.00	200,000.00	180,000.00
Direct labour	35,000.00	28,000.00	21,000.00
Overheads absorbed	208,334.00	166,667.20	125,000.40
Total cost	**443,334.00**	**394,667.20**	**326,000.40**
Unit cost (rounded)	4.43	4.93	5.43

£350,000/58,000 = £6.034 per machine hour
White = 20,000 × £6.034 = £120,680
Green = 20,000 × £6.034 = £120,680
Blue = 18,000 × £6.034 = £108,612

Receiving and storage

£45,000/10 = £4,500 per receipt
£45,000 − £4,500 (just white) = £40,500
£40,500/3 = £13,500
White = £4,500 + £13,500 = £18,000
Green = £13,500
Blue = £13,500

Packing

Output = white 100,000 + green 80,000 + blue 60,000 = 240,000
50,000/240,000 = £0.208 per overall
White = 100,000 × £0.208 = £20,800
Green = 80,000 × £0.208 = £16,640
Blue = 60,000 × £0.208 = £12,480 (see Table 11.5)

It can be seen from Table 11.5 that a much more balanced product cost is achieved with the various uses of the activities being reflected in the cost. It is not just the difference in the direct materials cost that gives the difference in product cost (see Table 11.6).

TABLE 11.5 Activity-Based Costing

	White £	Green £	Blue £
Direct materials	200,000	200,000	180,000
Direct labour	35,000	28,000	21,000
Overheads:			
Set-ups	27,500	16,500	11,000
Machine/Supervision	120,680	120,680	108,612
Receiving	18,000	13,500	13,500
Packing	20,800	16,640	12,480
Total cost	421,980	395,320	346,592
Unit cost (rounded)	4.22	4.94	5.78

TABLE 11.6   Summary—Comparison of Traditional Costing versus ABC

	White	Green	Blue
Traditional costing	£4.43	£4.93	£5.43
ABC	£4.22	£4.94	£5.78

Illustration of ABC for a Service Provider

Sancho Ltd source men's tailored suits from factories in the Shanghai region of China and supply them to retailers in the UK. Although they supply a product they essentially provide services—sourcing, quality management, warehousing, transport and distribution. They purchase from integrated factories in China that are producing an Italian look with their tailoring.

In the coming period they are sourcing four styles in a range of fabrics and sizes, with a negotiated price per style for retail operations across the UK (see Tables 11.7, 11.8, and 11.9).

TABLE 11.7

	Style A	Style B	Style C	Style D
Purchase price	£20.00	£25.00	£28.00	£30.00
Volume in the period	25,000	20,000	15,000	5,000
Customers	20	10	6	4

TABLE 11.8   Other Costs Incurred

Activity	Amount	Cost Driver
Sourcing in China	£45,500	Per quantity of garments purchased
Transportation/ Warehousing/Air freight from China	£80,000	
UK warehousing and distribution	£50,000	
Total	£175,500	

Continued

TABLE 11.8 *(Continued)*

Activity	Amount	Cost Driver
Quality inspections	£7,800	Number of inspections (1 per 500 garments)
Staff and associated costs in UK	£80,000	Per customer
Currency transfer costs Currency exchange costs	£5,000	In proportion to cost of garment purchases

TABLE 11.9 Costs Based on an ABC Approach

	Style A £	Style B £	Style C £	Style D £
Purchases	500,000	500,000	420,000	150,000
Sourcing/ Transportation	67,500	54,000	40,500	13,500
Quality inspection	3,000	2,400	1,800	600
UK staff	40,000	20,000	12,000	8,000
Currency transfer	1,592	1,592	1,338	478
Total cost	**612,092**	**577,992**	**475,638**	**172,578**
Unit cost	24.48	28.90	31.71	34.52

Advantages and Disadvantages of ABC

Advantages

- ABC provides a means of relating overheads to product where methods of manufacture have become more advanced and production is not so reliant on direct labour.
- It enables the business to see the activities that create overhead cost rather than just allocate those costs.
- It provides a system of costing that is relevant to service industries as well as manufacturers.
- It allows the business to be creative in determining its cost drivers.
- It may assist in the budgeting of the business through use of activity cost pools.

Disadvantages

- Deciding when the business should change from a traditional costing system to ABC is not clear-cut and may involve something of a leap of faith in taking on a hitherto untried system. Parallel running may be needed for a time.
- Determination of the cost drivers for a service industry might be difficult, as making the relationship to the service provided may not be easy.
- At the outset there may be a temptation to use a lot of cost drivers that make the costing rather complex, though it should be born in mind that a restricted number of cost drivers are unlikely to have the desired improvement.
- It may be necessary to change the budgeting system the business uses to fall in line with the activity cost pools.

Activity-Based Budgeting

Where a business has adopted ABC it will make sense to bring their budgeting in line with activity cost pools and cost drivers. If, as mentioned in Chapter 9, a budget is a financial plan of action, then that plan needs to reflect the other accounting methods that the business has adopted.

By monitoring the overheads related to their cost drivers, in the longer term the business will be able to control its costs by identifying non–value added activities that the business engages in.

Exercises and Activities

1. Give reasons why ABC may give more realistic product costs in a manufacturing situation.
2. A clothing manufacturer has identified four cost pools with their respective cost drivers (see Exercise Table 11.1).

EXERCISE TABLE 11.1

Cost Pool	Cost Driver
Machine activity	Machine hours
Quality inspection/control	Number of inspections required
Receiving of materials and handling	Number of receipts
Distribution	Per customer

Analyse the list of activity costs in Exercise Table 11.2 into their appropriate cost pools.

EXERCISE TABLE 11.2

Activity Cost	Cost Pool
Depreciation of machinery	
Van drivers' wages	
Receiving department wages	
Van running costs	
Quality control staff wages	
Machine maintenance costs	
Spare part required for machine	
Quality control staff training	
Packing costs	
Power costs of machinery	
Machine supervision costs	
Materials storage costs	
Fabric testing costs	
Machine cleaning costs	

3. A clothing manufacturer has identified the support activity costs listed in Exercise Table 11.3. Suggest suitable cost drivers.

EXERCISE TABLE 11.3

Cost	Cost Driver
Machine maintenance	
Set-up and recalibration costs	
Quality inspection	
Purchasing costs	
Machine supervision	
Despatch costs	

4. Great Activity Ltd produces four ranges of garments (A, B, C, D) in various sizes, colours and quantities. Exercise Table 11.4 shows the schedule for the coming period.

EXERCISE TABLE 11.4

	A	B	C	D
Number of production runs	4	5	3	3
Output	10,000	8,000	6,000	5,000
Direct materials cost per garment	£4.50	£3.80	£6.20	£5.60
Direct labour cost per garment	£1.30	£1.30	£1.65	£1.65
Machine hours per garment	0.15	0.20	0.25	0.25

A set-up is required each time a new production run is started. Overhead costs are as shown in Exercise Table 11.5.

EXERCISE TABLE 11.5

Cost	Amount £	Cost Driver
Set-up costs	19,500	Number of set-ups
Machine activity	35,000	Machine hours
Materials receiving and handling	12,000	Number of production runs
Packing/Despatch	15,000	Output

(a) Calculate the total cost for each range over the period and the unit cost of each of the garments, absorbing the overheads based on percentage of direct labour cost.
(b) Calculate the total cost for each range over the period and the unit cost using an ABC approach.
(c) Show the comparison of unit costs, traditionally and with ABC.

Drury, C. (2003), *Cost and Management Accounting: An Introduction* (5th edn), London: Thomson Learning.

Drury, C. (2005), *Management Accounting for Business Decisions* (3rd edn), London: Thomson Learning.

Drury, C. (2008), *Management and Cost Accounting* (7th edn), London: Thomson Learning.

Horngren, C. T., Sundem, G. L., and Stratton, W. O. (2008), *Introduction to Management Accounting* (14th edn), Harlow: Pearson Prentice Hall.

Kaplan, R. S., and Cooper, R. (1998), *Cost and Effect,* Boston: Harvard Business School Press.

Lucey, T. (2009), *Costing* (7th edn), London: Cengage Learning.

Russell, D., Patel, A., and Wilkinson-Riddle, G. (2002), *Cost Accounting: An Essential Guide,* Harlow: Prentice Hall.

12

CAPITAL INVESTMENT DECISIONS

Introduction

Though not strictly an aspect of costing, capital investment is an area in which fashion students may get involved when they go into employment in the industry. Therefore you will find it useful to have some understanding of the principles. Essentially capital investment decisions relate to the expenditure of large sums of money to fund capital projects. These might include the purchase of new equipment or a new computer system, or opening a new distribution centre or retail outlet—the types of projects are endless. The issue is that they involve spending large amounts of the company's capital, borrowing large sums of money or a combination of the two.

In most cases such projects will have some kind of technical assessment made of them, and the technical specification will be important in the decision-making process. However, projects will usually also require some kind of financial appraisal to assess their financial viability. This is known as *capital investment appraisal*. Several methodologies can be adopted to make this appraisal, but all rely on good information about the project and good estimates of how the project will perform.

The Capital Cost

The capital cost of the project is essentially the outlay to be made, though it may be a composite cost. Although is often made at the outset of the project, it may be paid in stages. The capital cost includes all the costs involved in getting the project up and running.

Example

A company has decided to invest in a new integrated computer system. In order to get the system up and running the following costs would be incurred:

- The hardware costs—PCs, visual display units, keyboards, server
- Installation costs—wiring for the network

- Building alterations costs to accommodate the network server
- Software and programming costs
- Staff training costs to enable staff to operate the system

Where a project involves large-scale building works, the capital cost may be paid in stages as the work progresses, and the plan will usually indicate the stages at which payments are to be made. The final payment is not made until the building has been handed over and any initial problems (known as *snags*) are resolved.

Accounting Rate of Return

Accounting rate of return (ARR) is one of the simplest methods of appraising capital investment decisions. It does, however, have limited application. This method considers the average profit that a project will generate over its life and compares that profit with the capital outlay.

Example

A company intends to spend £12,000 on a project that has a four-year life. Over the four years the project is expected to generate profit in each year (see Table 12.1).

Average profit for the project: £5,600/4 = £1,400
ARR of the project = (£1,400/£12,000) × 100 = 11.67%

TABLE 12.1

Year	Profit £
1	1,200
2	1,400
3	1,600
4	1,400
Total	£5,600

In making the decision based on this method, management would be looking for the highest-percentage return. Note that there is no standard way of calculating the ARR; the preceding is just an illustration of one method. The figures have been kept simple in this example to illustrate the method, but in reality capital investment decisions usually involve very large sums of money.

This method of appraisal is clearly simple and has a logic that we can all relate to in that we want a higher return from our capital outlay. However, it has limited application. For most projects it will be difficult to assess how much profit the individual project has earned because profit tends to be calculated for the whole business or individual operations and not single projects. So if a manufacturer decided to purchase a new laser cutter, it might be difficult to establish how much profit that single piece of equipment has generated. It may have application where the project is to open a new outlet that will generate identifiable profits, but it then calls into question whether profit is the best measure of capital investment.

Net Cash Inflows

Other than the accounting rate of return, most other methods of capital investment appraisal use cash flows rather than profit as the measure. These have the advantage of being much more identifiable with the project in terms of both inflows and outflows. The *cash inflows* are the revenues that the project generates. The *cash outflows* are the expenses and costs of the project. These are netted off to give net cash inflows. The shape of the net cash inflows over the life of the project are interesting in that they are similar to the shape of product life cycles and tell us something about the project in question.

Figure 12.1a illustrates the net cash inflows for a project. They take a little time to get going but once the project is under way they plateau out and eventually fall as the project comes to the end of its useful life. The steeper the initial rise, the quicker the project gets under way (shorter lead time); the flatter the initial rise, the longer the lead time. A long plateau indicates a project with a long life span, whereas a short plateau indicates a short project that quickly comes to the end of its useful life (see Figures 12.1b and 12.1c).

Payback Period

The payback period method of capital investment appraisal uses net cash inflows as just described and is probably the most commonly used method of investment appraisal. The thinking behind the method is, 'How quickly will the business get the capital investment back from the project?' So again we have a method with an easily understandable logic that we can all relate to. The decision rule in the payback period method is to look for the shortest payback period, i.e. the project that will repay the capital outlay the quickest. This is done by estimating the net cash inflows over the life of the project and making them cumulative year on year. It is then established when the cumulative net cash inflows will reach the capital cost.

A General shape of the net cash inflows

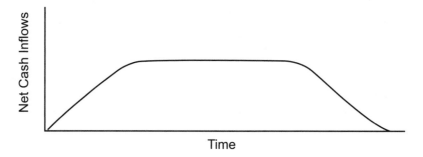

B Shape where the project has minimal lead time

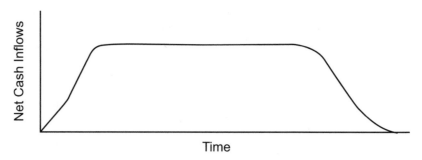

C Shape where the project has a long lead time

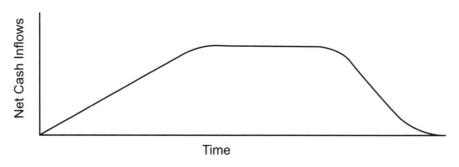

Figure 12.1 Net cash inflow shapes.

Example

A clothing manufacturer has decided to invest in a computer-controlled laser cutter at a capital cost of £150,000. It is estimated that this system will serve the company for six years, at the end of which it will be obsolete. It is estimated that it will produce the following net cash inflows over the six-year period (see Table 12.2).

TABLE 12.2

	Inflows £	Cumulative inflows £
Year 1	45,000	45,000
Year 2	65,000	110,000
Year 3	80,000	190,000
Year 4	80,000	270,000
Year 5	80,000	350,000
Year 6	65,000	415,000

It can be seen from the cumulative column in Table 12.2 that the capital cost is not matched by net cash inflows until sometime during the third year of the project. By the end of year 3 the cumulative net cash inflows will have reached £190,000, exceeding the capital cost. Thus the payback period is two years plus a fraction of year 3.

It can be seen that at the end of year 2 the cumulative net cash inflows are £110,000; thus a further £40,000 is required to match the capital cost of £150,000, and that £40,000 will come from the £80,000 generated in year 3. The fraction is therefore as follows:

$$£40,000/£80,000 = 0.5$$

The payback period is therefore 2.5 years.

Where this laser cutter is compared with other similar systems, the shortest payback period would be selected.

This is also a simple method of calculation and is based on the concept that the business would want to know how quickly they would get their investment back. However, it has two major shortcomings in that it does not take account of the changing value of money, nor does it recognize that some projects take much longer to get established but in the longer term may be more profitable than one with a shorter lead time.

Discounted Cash Flow

A better way to look at capital investment appraisal is to use *discounted cash flow* (DCF) and to calculate the *net present value* (NPV) for the project. DCF works on the basis of compounded interest, only in reverse.

If you had £100 to invest and you could get 5 per cent per annum interest on your investment, then after one year you would have £105. DCF works on the basis that future income given at a rate of interest will be worth less today than in the future. Thus, using the preceding example, if we take the £105 as future income, then today (at the beginning of the investment) it is worth £100, known as its *present value*.

The present values of future income and expenditure can be calculated using present value factor tables. Table 12.3 provides an extract; a more detailed table is at the end of this chapter.

TABLE 12.3 Present Value Factors

Year	3%	4%	5%	6%	10%	12%
1	0.9709	0.9615	0.9524	0.9434	0.9091	0.8929
2	0.9426	0.9426	0.9070	0.8900	0.8264	0.7972
3	0.9151	0.8890	0.8638	0.8396	0.7513	0.7118
4	0.8885	0.8548	0.8227	0.7921	0.6830	0.6355
5	0.8626	0.8219	0.7835	0.7473	0.6209	0.5674
6	0.8375	0.7903	0.7462	0.7050	0.5645	0.5066

Take the appropriate rate of interest and read off the factor against the year. The factor is multiplied by the future income (or expenditure) to give the present value of that income (or expenditure).

$$£105 \times 0.9524 = £100$$

A decision has to be made with respect to the interest rate to use. Many businesses would choose their current rate of interest on their borrowing, or perhaps an average rate if they have several loans at different rates of interest. One school of thought, however, suggests that the weighted average cost of capital should be used, taking into account any notional dividends on share capital as well as rates of interest. Alternatively, more than one interest rate could be used to show a range of circumstances.

Example

Taking the example of the laser cutter used previously, assuming a rate of interest of 10 per cent would give the results shown in Table 12.4.

The present values of the net cash inflows are then totalled up for the whole project and the capital cost is deducted to give the net present value of the project. In this example that would be as shown in Table 12.5.

The decision rule in using net present value is to choose the highest NPV and to rule out any negative NPVs. The highest NPV indicates the highest return against the capital cost once future income has been converted to its present value.

Discounted Payback Period

Payback period and discounted cash flow can be combined in the discounted payback period method. Here the simplicity of payback period is tempered with the harder edge of discounted cash flow. The inflows are discounted to give their present values and the present

TABLE 12.4

	Inflows £	PV Factor at 10%	Present Value £ (rounded)
Year 1	45,000	0.9091	40,910
Year 2	65,000	0.8264	53,716
Year 3	80,000	0.7513	60,104
Year 4	80,000	0.6830	54,640
Year 5	80,000	0.6209	49,672
Year 6	65,000	0.5645	36,693

TABLE 12.5

Total present values	£295,735
Capital cost made at start	£150,000
Net present value	**£145,735**

values made cumulative to determine when the cumulative present values match the capital cost (see Table 12.6).

You can see from the table that the project's discounted net cash inflows will match the capital cost in year 3, as before, but much nearer to the end of the year.

TABLE 12.6

	Inflows £	PV Factor at 10%	Present Value £ (rounded)	Cumulative Present Values £
Year 1	45,000	0.9091	40,910	40,910
Year 2	65,000	0.8264	53,716	94,626
Year 3	80,000	0.7513	60,104	154,730
Year 4	80,000	0.6830	54,640	209,370
Year 5	80,000	0.6209	49,672	259,042
Year 6	65,000	0.5645	36,693	295,735

At the end of year 2 a further £55,374 is required to match the capital cost (£150,000–£94,626) that will have to come out of the discounted inflows for year 3.

$$£55,374/£60,104 = 0.92$$

Therefore the discounted payback period is 2.92 years (almost three years).

Though this is better than the straight payback period, the decision rule is the same, i.e. look for the shortest discounted payback period. It therefore does not take into account projects that have long lead times but are ultimately more profitable for the business.

Illustration

Progressive Ltd is a fashion design house and is considering investing in some high-tech equipment. They are considering two alternative plans:

Plan 1—the Micro-Spot System
Plan 2—the Gruber System

Both have different capital costs, and because they work in slightly different ways they have different lead times—hence different net cash inflows in years 1 and 2. However, they are both estimated to have a life of around five years, after which something new is likely to have become available. At the end of the five years the supplier of the Gruber System guarantees a minimum residual value (scrap value) of £10,000. This has been added to the final year's net cash inflows.

The company's current average capital cost is running at 12 per cent per annum and it is decided to discount at this rate (see Table 12.7).

TABLE 12.7

	Plan 1 Micro-Spot	Plan 2 Gruber
Cost	£230,000	£280,000
Life	5 years	5 years
Net cash inflows		
Year 1	£40,000	£60,000
Year 2	£80,000	£100,000
Year 3	£100,000	£100,000
Year 4	£60,000	£60,000
Year 5	£50,000	£60,000

TABLE 12.8

Year	Net Cash Inflows Micro-Spot	Cumulative	Net Cash Inflows Gruber	Cumulative
1	£40,000	£40,000	£60,000	£60,000
2	£80,000	£120,000	£100,000	£160,000
3	£100,000	£220,000	£100,000	£260,000
4	£60,000	£280,000	£60,000	£320,000
5	£50,000	£330,000	£60,000	£380,000

Payback Period

Micro Spot System—payback period is 3.17 years

At the end of year 3 the cumulative net cash inflows are £220,000 leaving a further £10,000 required from year 4 to match the capital cost (see Table 12.8).

$$10,000/60,000 = 0.17; \text{ thus } 3.17 \text{ years}$$

Gruber system—payback period is 3.33 years

At the end of year 3 the cumulative net cash inflows are £260,000 leaving a further £20,000 required from year 4 to match the capital cost.

$$20,000/60,000 = 0.33; \text{ thus } 3.33 \text{ years}$$

Plan 1, the Micro Spot System, has marginally the shortest payback period, 3.17 years (see Table 12.9), whereas Plan 2, the Gruber System has a 3.33-year payback period (see Table 12.10). So on the basis of that methodology, the Micro-Spot System would be chosen.

On the basis of net present value, the Micro-Spot System has a positive NPV of £7,168, whereas the Gruber System has a negative NPV of £(3,352). So on the basis of NPV the Micro-Spot System would be preferable.

You could now use this illustration to establish the discounted payback period for the two plans.

Conclusions

Capital investment decisions are about spending large sums of money on equipment, facilities, buildings and the like that will have a life over several years. The objective is to estimate which plan will provide the business with the most financially viable option.

TABLE 12.9   Net Present Value: Micro-Spot System

Year	Net Cash Inflows Micro-Spot £	PV Factor at 12%	Present Value £
1	40,000	0.8929	35,712
2	80,000	0.7972	63,776
3	100,000	0.7118	71,180
4	60,000	0.6355	38,130
5	50,000	0.5674	28,370
Total present values			237,168
Capital cost			230,000
Net present value			7,168

TABLE 12.10   Net Present Value: Gruber System

Year	Net Cash Inflows Gruber £	PV Factor at 12%	Present Value £
1	60,000	0.8929	53,574
2	100,000	0.7972	79,720
3	100,000	0.7118	71,180
4	60,000	0.6355	38,130
5	60,000	0.5674	34,044
Total present values			276,648
Capital cost			280,000
Net present value			(3,352)

The calculations used will be only as good as the estimated data provided. Therefore care needs to be taken in assembling the information.

In this chapter four methods of capital investment appraisal have been considered:

1. Accounting rate of return
2. Payback period
3. Discounted cash flow using net present value
4. Discounted payback period

The decision rules for the four methods are as follows:

1. Accounting rate of return—select the highest average percentage return on the capital expenditure.
2. Payback period—select the shortest.
3. Net present value—eliminate any negative NPVs and select the highest positive NPV.
4. Discounted payback period—select the shortest.

Exercises and Activities

1. Ambladec Ltd are working on a project that will last three years at a capital cost of £400,000. The net cash inflows are estimated to be as follows:
   Year 1: £100,000
   Year 2: £200,000
   Year 3: £300,000
   Calculate the payback period and net present value assuming a discount rate of 15 per cent.
2. Examine the net cash inflows listed in Exercise Table 12.1 for three capital projects and then respond to the following.

EXERCISE TABLE 12.1

Year	Project 1 Net Cash Inflows	Project 2 Net Cash Inflows	Project 3 Net Cash Inflows
1	40,000	80,000	60,000
2	65,000	100,000	70,000
3	68,000	90,000	70,000
4	70,000	80,000	70,000
5	60,000	70,000	70,000
6	40,000	50,000	50,000

(a) Sketch the shape of the net cash inflows for the three projects.
(b) Which projects have the shortest lead time?
(c) Which project maintains its revenues the longest?
(d) Which project barely plateaus out in terms of revenues?

3. Provinces Ltd are considering opening a new fashion store in Merborough. They are looking at two possible town centre venues with the costs and revenues shown in Exercise Tables 12.2–12.5.
   Location 1: A unit in the new Merborough shopping center

EXERCISE TABLE 12.2

Capital Costs	£
Cost of 3 years' lease (paid up front)	234,000
Initial legal fees	3,500
Shop fitting	120,000

EXERCISE TABLE 12.3

Revenues and Revenue Expenses	Revenues £	Revenue Expenses £
Year 1	280,000	100,000
Year 2	400,000	110,000
Year 3	440,000	120,000

Location 2: A shop unit on King Street

EXERCISE TABLE 12.4

Capital Costs	£
Cost of 3 years' lease (paid up front)	255,000
Initial legal fees	4,500
Shop fitting	130,000

EXERCISE TABLE 12.5

Revenues and Revenue Expenses	Revenues £	Revenue Expenses £
Year 1	280,000	120,000
Year 2	420,000	140,000
Year 3	480,000	150,000

Make an appraisal of the two options being considered using the following methods:

    (a) Payback period

    (b) Net present value based on discounting at 10 per cent

    (c) Discounted payback period, also based on discounting at 10 per cent

Based on your reasoning, outline which location gives the best appraisal.

4.   Ember Holdings are considering purchasing a new computer-driven machine. The company supplying the machine have suggested that Ember Holdings could have it for four years, after the supplier would buy it back for £4,000. Alternatively the machine could be productive for six years, but at the end of six years the supplier would not want it back and it would have no scrap value. The capital cost of the machine is £24,000 and the estimated net cash inflows are as shown in Exercise Table 12.6.

    Evaluate the two options using both payback period and NPV. Use a discount rate of 12 per cent.

EXERCISE TABLE 12.6

Year 1	£4,000
Year 2	£6,500
Year 3	£10,000
Year 4	£9,000
Year 5	£2,000
Year 6	£1,500

5.   Ember Holdings (from the preceding example), having done some further research, have found a similar machine, known as 'Q', that would do the job and has a lower initial capital cost of only £16,800. However, the Q machine has an expected life of only three years, at the end of which it would have to be scrapped. If the project is to continue for six years, an identical machine will have to be purchased at the beginning of year 4 at an estimated cost of £18,000. Evaluate machine Q using a discount rate of 12 per cent, and compare to your result your evaluations from Exercise 4.

Further Reading

Drury, C. (2003), *Cost and Management Accounting: An Introduction* (5th edn), London: Thomson Learning.

Drury, C. (2005), *Management Accounting for Business Decisions* (3rd edn), London: Thomson Learning.

Drury, C. (2008), *Management and Cost Accounting* (7th edn), London: Thomson Learning.

Horngren, C. T., Sundem, G. L., and Stratton, W. O. (2008), *Introduction to Management Accounting* (14th edn), Harlow: Pearson Prentice Hall.

Russell, D., Patel, A., and Wilkinson-Riddle, G. (2002), *Cost Accounting: An Essential Guide,* Harlow: Prentice Hall.

Present Value Factor Table

Year	1%	2%	3%	4%	5%	6%	7%	8%	9%	10%	12%	14%	15%
1	0.9901	0.9804	0.9709	0.9615	0.9524	0.9434	0.9346	0.9259	0.9174	0.9091	0.8929	0.8772	0.8696
2	0.9803	0.9612	0.9426	0.9426	0.9070	0.8900	0.8734	0.8573	0.8417	0.8264	0.7972	0.7695	0.7561
3	0.9706	0.9423	0.9151	0.8890	0.8638	0.8396	0.8163	0.7938	0.7722	0.7513	0.7118	0.6750	0.6575
4	0.9610	0.9238	0.8885	0.8548	0.8227	0.7921	0.7629	0.7350	0.7084	0.6830	0.6355	0.5921	0.5718
5	0.9515	0.9057	0.8626	0.8219	0.7835	0.7473	0.7130	0.6806	0.6499	0.6209	0.5674	0.5194	0.4972
6	0.9420	0.8880	0.8375	0.7903	0.7462	0.7050	0.6663	0.6302	0.5963	0.5645	0.5066	0.4556	0.4323
7	0.9327	0.8706	0.8131	0.7599	0.7107	0.6651	0.6227	0.5835	0.5470	0.5132	0.4523	0.3996	0.3759
8	0.9235	0.8535	0.7894	0.7307	0.6768	0.6274	0.5820	0.5403	0.5019	0.4665	0.4039	0.3506	0.3269
9	0.9143	0.8368	0.7664	0.7026	0.6446	0.5919	0.5439	0.5002	0.4604	0.4241	0.3606	0.3075	0.2843
10	0.9053	0.8203	0.7441	0.6756	0.6139	0.5584	0.5083	0.4632	0.4224	0.3855	0.3220	0.2697	0.2472

Year	16%	18%	20%	21%	22%	24%	25%	28%	30%	32%	34%	35%	40%
1	0.8621	0.8475	0.8333	0.8264	0.8197	0.8065	0.8000	0.7813	0.7692	0.7576	0.7463	0.7407	0.7143
2	0.7432	0.7182	0.6944	0.6830	0.6719	0.6504	0.6400	0.6104	0.5917	0.5739	0.5569	0.5487	0.5102
3	0.6407	0.6086	0.5787	0.5645	0.5507	0.5245	0.5120	0.4768	0.4552	0.4348	0.4156	0.4064	0.3644
4	0.5523	0.5158	0.4823	0.4665	0.4514	0.4230	0.4096	0.3725	0.3501	0.3294	0.3102	0.3011	0.2603
5	0.4761	0.4371	0.4019	0.3855	0.3700	0.3411	0.3277	0.2910	0.2693	0.2495	0.2315	0.2230	0.1859
6	0.4104	0.3704	0.3349	0.3186	0.3033	0.2751	0.2621	0.2274	0.2072	0.1890	0.1727	0.1652	0.1328
7	0.3538	0.3139	0.2791	0.2633	0.2486	0.2218	0.2097	0.1776	0.1594	0.1432	0.1289	0.1224	0.0949
8	0.3050	0.2660	0.2326	0.2176	0.2038	0.1789	0.1678	0.1388	0.1226	0.1085	0.0962	0.0906	0.0678
9	0.2630	0.2255	0.1938	0.1799	0.1670	0.1443	0.1342	0.1084	0.0943	0.0822	0.0718	0.0671	0.0484
10	0.2267	0.1911	0.1615	0.1486	0.1369	0.1164	0.1074	0.0847	0.0725	0.0623	0.0536	0.0497	0.0346

BIBLIOGRAPHY

Bhimani, A., Horngren, C. T, and Datar, S. M. (2008), *Management and Cost Accounting* (4th edn), Harlow: Prentice Hall.

Bromwich, M., and Bhimani, A. (1997), *Management Accounting: Pathways to Progress*, CIMA.

Brown, P. (2001), *Ready Wear Apparel Analysis* (3rd edn), Harlow: Prentice Hall.

Carr, H., and Latham, B. (2008), *Carr and Latham's Technology of Clothing Manufacture* (4th edn), revised by Tyler, D., Oxford: Blackwell.

Chuter, A. J. (1995), *Introduction to Clothing Production Management* (2nd edn), Oxford: Blackwell Science.

Cooklin, G. (1997), *Garment Technology for Fashion Designers*, Oxford: Blackwell Science.

Cooklin, G. (2006), *Introduction to Clothing Manufacture*, revised by Hayes, S. G., and McLoughlin, J., Oxford: Blackwell Science.

Drury, C. (2003), *Cost and Management Accounting: An Introduction* (5th edn), London: Thomson Learning.

Drury, C. (2005), *Management Accounting for Business Decisions* (3rd edn), London: Thomson Learning.

Drury, C. (2008), *Management and Cost Accounting* (7th edn), London: Thomson Learning.

Easey, M. (2009) *Fashion Marketing* (3rd edn), Oxford: Wiley-Blackwell.

Fairhurst, C., ed. (2008), *Advances in Apparel Production,* Cambridge: Woodhead.

Horngren, C. T., et al. (2008), *Introduction to Management Accounting* (14th edn), Harlow, Pearson Prentice Hall.

J. & P. Coats Limited (1996), *The Technology of Seams and Threads,* Glasgow: Coats Ltd.

Jackson, T. and Shaw, D. (2006), *The Fashion Handbook,* London: Routledge.

Jackson, T. and Shaw, D. (2009), *Mastering Fashion Marketing*, London: Macmillan.

Jones, R. M. (2006), *The Apparel Industry* (2nd edn), Oxford: Blackwell.

Lucey, T. (2005), *Management Accounting* (5th edn), London: Continuum.

Lucey, T. (2009), *Costing* (7th edn), London: Cengage Learning.

Mintzberg, H., Quinn, J. B., and Ghoshal, S. (1998), *The Strategy Process: Revised European Edition* (2nd edn), Harlow: Prentice Hall.

Russell, D., Patel, A., and Wilkinson-Riddle, G. (2002), *Cost Accounting: An Essential Guide,* Harlow: Prentice Hall.

Ryan, B. (2004), *Finance and Accounting for Business,* London: Thomson.

Tyler, D. (1991), *Materials Management in Clothing Production,* Oxford: Blackwell Science.

Wood, F., and Sangster, A. (2008), *Frank Wood's Business Accounting 1* (11th edn), Harlow: Financial Times/ Prentice Hall.

ANSWERS TO EXERCISES

Chapter 2

EXERCISE TABLE 2.1

Direct Materials	Direct Labour	Direct Expenses
b	a	e
d	c	j
f	h	l
g	k	r
i	p	
m		
n		
o		
q		
s		

EXERCISE TABLE 2.2

Direct Materials	Direct Labour	Direct Expenses	Production Overhead	Non-Production Overhead
a	b	r	d	i
c	e	u	g	j (packing large scale for distribution)
j (material for a packed product)	f		h	
l	j (labour for a packed product)		o	k
n	p		s	m
x	y		t	o
			v	q
				s
				w
				z

Note some costs may be in more than one category

EXERCISE TABLE 2.3

Indirect Materials	Indirect Labour	Indirect Expenses
a	b	e
f	c	g
k	d	h
o	i	j
p	l	
	m	
	n	

EXERCISE TABLE 2.4

Selling and Distribution Costs	Administration Costs	Finance Expenses
a	c	e
b	d	f
i	g	h
k	j	n
l	m	
	o	
	p	

Chapter 3

EXERCISE TABLE 3.1

BERN HEART FASHIONS PERIOD COST REPORT AUGUST 200X

	£	£
Opening stock of direct materials		2,500
Add purchases of direct materials		86,700
		89,200
Less closing stock of direct materials		2,800
Cost of Materials consumed		86,400
Cutting room wages	2,300	
Sewing room wages	3,500	
Press and finishing wages	2,580	
Direct labour cost		8,380
Prime cost		94,780
Factory supervisors' wages	3,800	
Heat, light and power (factory)	3,150	
Insurances (factory)	188	
Depreciation:		
Factory equipment	350	
Production overheads		7,488
		102,268
Add opening work-in-progress		4,250
		106,518
Less closing work-in-progress		4,350
Production cost		102,168
Administration salaries	2,680	
Heat, light and power (office)	1,050	
Insurance (office)	62	
Bank charges	120	
Nonproduction overheads		3912
Total cost		**£106,080**

EXERCISE TABLE 3.2   Spring Garments period cost report May 200Y

	£	£
Opening stock of direct materials		7,800
Add purchases of direct materials		88,000
Add carriage inwards		230
		96,030
Less returns of direct materials		340
		95,690
Less closing stock of direct materials		9,200
direct materials consumed		86,490
Cutting room wages	4,400	
Sewing machinists' wages	8,600	
Press and finish wages	3,200	
Direct labour costs		16,200
Prime cost		102,690
Factory supervisors' wages	4,500	
Cleaning costs (factory)	4,800	
Rent and business rates (factory)	4,480	
Insurances (factory)	200	
Sundry expenses	130	
Depreciation:		
Factory machinery, furniture & fittings	1,500	
Production overhead		15,610
		118,300
Add opening work-in-progress		5,600
		123,900
Less closing work-in-progress		6,200
Production cost		117,700
Administration wages	2,250	
Cleaning costs (office)	1,600	
Rent and business rates (office)	1,120	
Insurance (office)	50	
Postage and stationery	380	
Bank charges and interest	420	
		5,820
Total cost		**£123,520**

EXERCISE TABLE 3.3 Analysis of direct materials October 200Z

	Grey PC £	Blue Denim £	Plain Calico £	White Cotton £	Blue Cotton £	Inter £	Buttons £	Thread £	Zips £
Opening stock	320	2,100	2,200	2,100	1,350	3,400	1,050	860	380
Purchases	3,500	4,200	2,500	2,500	—	1,600	680	1,200	—
Carriage in	125	—	80	—	—	—	—	—	—
	3,945	6,380	4,700	4,600	1,350	5,000	1,730	2,060	380
Closing stock	480	1,200	860	1,400	1,250	2,250	340	250	380
Direct materials consumed	3,465	5,180	3,840	3,200	100	2,750	340	250	—

Chapter 4

EXERCISE TABLE 4.1 Mercia Fashions

Direct materials			
Fabric	20,000 × 1.4	@ £5.20	145,600.00
Zips	20,000	@ £0.45	9,000.00
Buttons	20,000 × 3	@ £0.01	600.00
Interlining	20,000	@ £0.25	5,000.00
Thread	20.000	@ £0.20	4,000.00
Direct material costs			**164,200.00**
Direct labour			
Laying up & cutting	3 × 6	@ £11.05	198.90
Fusing	4	@ £6.25	25.00
Sewing	20,000 × 10/60	@ £6.75	22,500.00
Pressing	20,000 × 0.5/60	@ £7.15	1,191.67
Packing	20,000 × 0.4/60	@ £6.25	833.33
Direct labour cost			**24,748.90**
Production overhead			
Laying up & cutting	3 × 6	@ £15.20	273.60
Fusing	3 (MHR)	@ £6.70	20.10
Sewing	£22,500	@ 180%	40,500.00
Pressing	20,000 × 0.5/60	@ £7.60	1,266.67
Packing	£833.33	@ 150%	1,250.00
Production overhead cost			**43,310.37**
Production cost			232,259.27
Nonproduction overheads	£232,259.27	@ 5%	1,162.96
Total cost			**£233,422.23**
Unit cost			**£11.67**

EXERCISE TABLE 4.2 Frankfurt Fashions

	Cutting	Sewing	Press/Finish
Estimated overheads	£24,000	£96,000	£22,000
Service overheads:			
Maintenance	£6,500	£35,600	£6,700
Cleaning	£7,500	£23,400	£6,000
Personnel	£4,500	£25,500	£10,500
Total	£42,500	£180,500	£45,200
Direct labour hours	5,500	18,240	5,000
Machine hours	3,600	—	—
Direct labour cost	£71,000	£114,200	£33,500

Production overhead absorption rates

Cutting room

$$\frac{\text{Total overheads}}{\text{Machine hours}} \quad \frac{£42,500}{3,600} = £11.83 \text{ per machine hour}$$

Sewing room

$$\frac{\text{Total overheads}}{\text{Direct labour cost}} \quad \frac{£180,500}{£114,200} \times 100 = 158.06\% \text{ of direct labour cost}$$

Press/Finish

$$\frac{\text{Total overheads}}{\text{Direct labour hours}} \quad \frac{£45,200}{5,000} = £9.04 \text{ per direct labour hour}$$

Chapter 5

To calculate the number of garments per colour and size based on a given ratio follow these steps:

1. Take the total order quantity (3,600 pieces).
2. Add up all the ratios (20).
3. Divide the total order quantity by the total ratio (3,600/20 = 180).
4. Therefore a ratio of 1 equals 180 pieces and a ratio of 2 equals 360 pieces.

Colour/Size	10	12	14	16
Navy	180 pieces	180 pieces	180 pieces	180 pieces
Red	180 pieces	180 pieces	180 pieces	180 pieces
White	180 pieces	360 pieces	360 pieces	180 pieces
Black	180 pieces	360 pieces	360 pieces	180 pieces

Chapter 6

EXERCISE TABLE 6.1

Style Description	Order Quantity	Ship Date	Delivery Date	Sell Price Euro	Sell Price £	Factory Name	US$ Buy Price	£ Buy Price	Pack & Test Costs £	Freight Cost £	Total Garment Cost £	Gross profit £ / Gment	% Gment Margin	Total Sales £	Total Gross Profit £
Embroidered blouse	7,600	30-Jun	25-Aug	5.59	3.86	D	3.50	2.12	0.44	0.35	2.91	0.95	25	29,336.00	7,220.00
Pearl button blouse	3,000	30-Jun	25-Aug	3.99	2.75	C	2.20	1.33	0.44	0.35	2.12	0.63	23	8,250.00	1,890.00
Bow blouse	4,800	30-Jun	25-Aug	7.00	4.83	C	3.50	2.12	0.44	0.35	2.91	1.92	40	23,184.00	9,216.00
Gathered hem blouse	2,000	30-Jun	25-Aug	7.25	5.00	C	4.00	2.42	0.44	0.35	3.21	1.79	36	10,000.00	3,580.00
Applique blouse	5,600	30-Jun	25-Aug	5.75	3.97	D	3.75	2.27	0.44	0.35	3.06	0.91	23	22,232.00	5,096.00
	23,000												29	93,002.00	27,002.00
										Department overall total % margin					
US $															
Euros															

Chapter 7

EXERCISE TABLE 7.1

Cost	Fixed	Variable	Semi-Variable
Thread		✓	
Building insurance premiums	✓		
Heat/Light/Power			✓
Interlining		✓	
Shirt buttons		✓	
Factory manager's salary	✓		
Fusing press operator's wages		✓	
Business rates	✓		
Stationery	✓		
Telephone			✓
Cutting room wages		✓	
Receptionists' wages	✓		
Press room wages		✓	
Zips for trousers		✓	
Boxes for a boxed shirt		✓	
Delivery vehicle costs			✓
Canteen staff wages	✓		
Bank loan interest	✓		
Bank charges	✓		
Fabric for dresses		✓	

EXERCISE TABLE 7.2 Fallowfield Fashions

	Shirt LS £'000	Shirt SS £'000	Blouse A £'000	Blouse B £'000	Total £'000
Sales	200	160	90	150	600
Less variable costs	145	115	92	103	455
Contribution	55	45	(2)	47	145
Fixed costs					140
Net profit					5

If Fallowfield Fashion eliminate Blouse A from their range based on the current information they will lose the sales revenue of £90,000 but will also eliminate the variable costs of £92,000, thus eliminating the negative contribution of £2,000 and increasing the profit from £5,000 to £7,000.

EXERCISE TABLE 7.3 Melton Fashions

	A £	B £	C £	Total £
Confirmed business Sales	35,000	32,000	27,200	94,200
Less variable costs	26,600	22,400	21,600	70,600
Contribution	8,400	9,600	5,600	23,600
Fixed costs				20,000
Net profit				3,600
Possible additional business Sales (500 × £31)			15,500	
Less variable costs (500 × £27*)			13,500	
Additional contribution				2,000
Net profit if additional order accepted				5,600

*Variable cost per garment £21,600/800 = £27

Chapter 8

EXERCISE TABLE 8.1   Your Event Ltd

Production	Fixed Costs £	Variable Costs £	Total Costs £	Value of Sales £	Profit (Loss) £
0	32,000	0	32,000	0	(32,000)
1,000	32,000	48,000	80,000	56,000	(24,000)
2,000	32,000	96,000	128,000	112,000	(16,000)
3,000	32,000	144,000	176,000	168,000	(8,000)
4,000	32,000	192,000	224,000	224,000	BEP
5,000	32,000	240,000	272,000	280,000	8,000
6,000	32,000	288,000	320,000	336,000	16,000
7,000	32,000	336,000	368,000	392,000	24,000

BEP = £32,000 ÷ (8/56) = £224,000 sales
Or £224,000/£56 = 4,000 garments

EXERCISE TABLE 8.3   For every four garments that the business sells, three would raise £75 and one would raise £32. This would give a sales figure of £107 for each four garments (3 × £25 = £75 plus 1 × £32 = £107).
The variable costs of these four garments would be £24 × 4 = £96. Therefore the contribution would be £107 – £96 = £11.
BEP = £70,000 ÷ (£11/£107) = £680,910 sales, or approximately 25,456 jackets (figures rounded).

Production	FC	VC	TC	Sales	Profit (Loss)
25,456	70,000	610,944	680,944	75% 477,300 25% 203,648 Total 680,948	£4 Close

EXERCISE TABLE 8.4

	£
Variable costs (14,000 × £15)	210,000
Fixed costs	47,000
Total costs	257,000
Required profit	23,000
Sales	280,000

selling price per pair = £280,000/14,000 = £20 per pair

Chapter 9

EXERCISE TABLE 9.2 Debidall Ltd

	April £	May £	June £	July £	Aug £	Sept £
Budgeted receipts: Debtors	6,400	5,400	7,400	6,800	6,300	6,500
Budgeted expenses:						
Creditors	3,500	3,600	2,600	4,200	3,400	3,100
Wages & salaries	1,900	1,900	2,100	1,900	1,900	1,900
Heat, light, power		500			500	
Insurance				180		
Sundries	140	140	140	140	140	140
Total expenses	5,540	6,140	4,840	6,420	5,940	5,140
Net cash	860	(750)	2,560	380	360	1,360
Balance b/fwd	1,800	2,660	1,910	4,470	4,850	5,210
Balance c/fwd	2,660	1,910	4,470	4,850	5,210	6,570

EXERCISE TABLE 9.3 Flare Fashions Ltd

(i) Sales lag analysis

	Budgeted Sales	Oct £'000	Nov £'000	Dec £'000	Jan £'000	Feb £'000	Mar £'000	Apr £'000
October	1,200	600	552					
November	1,100		550	506				
December	1,000			500	460			
January	1,400				700	644		
February	1,200					600	552	
March	1,100						550	506
To cash budget			1,102	1,006	1,160	1,244	1,102	

(ii) Cash budget

	January £'000	February £'000	March £'000
Budgeted receipts—sales	1,160	1,244	1,102
Budgeted expenses: wages & salaries	60	60	60
Creditors	365	335	370
Variable overheads	196	175	196
Fixed overheads	200	161	200
Corporation tax	750		
Dividend			500
Capital expenditure	1,000		700
Total budgeted expenses	2,571	731	2,026
Net cash	(1,411)	513	(924)
Balance b/fwd	145	(1,266)	(753)
Balance c/fwd	(1,266)	(753)	(1,677)

EXERCISE TABLE 9.4

Materials price variance

$$420 \times (£3.25 - £3.30) = £(21) \text{ Adverse}$$
$$£3.25 \times (450 - 420) = £97.50 \text{ Favourable}$$
$$\text{Net variance} = £76.50 \text{ Favourable}$$

Wage rate variance

$$76 \times (£6.20 - £6.25) = £(3.80) \text{ Adverse}$$

Labour efficiency variance

$$£6.20 \times (75 - 76) = £(6.20) \text{ Adverse}$$
$$\text{Net variance} = £(10.00) \text{ Adverse}$$

Chapter 11

EXERCISE TABLE 11.2

Activity Cost	Cost Pool
Depreciation of machinery	Machine activity
Van drivers' wages	Distribution
Receiving department wages	Receiving
Van running costs	Distribution
Quality control staff wages	Quality inspection
Machine maintenance costs	Machine activity
Spare part required for machine	Machine activity
Quality control staff training	Quality inspection
Packing costs	Distribution
Power costs of machinery	Machine activity
Machine supervision costs	Machine activity
Material storage costs	Receiving
Fabric testing costs	Quality inspection
Machine cleaning costs	Machine activity

EXERCISE TABLE 11.3

Cost	Cost Driver
Machine maintenance	Machine hours
Set-up and recalibration costs	Number of set-ups
Quality inspection	Production/Output
Purchasing costs	Volume of orders
Machine supervision	Machine hours
Despatch costs	Output

EXERCISE TABLE 11.4   Great Activity Ltd

(a) Absorption cost—based on percentage of direct labour

	A £	B £	C £	D £
Direct materials cost	45,000	30,400	37,200	28,000
Direct labour cost	13,000	10,400	9,900	8,250
Overheads	25,506	20,405	19,424	16,187
Total cost	83,506	61,205	66,524	52,437
Unit cost	£8.35	£7.65	£11.09	£10.49

(b) ABC approach

	A £	B £	C £	D £
Direct materials cost	45,000	30,400	37,200	28,000
Direct labour cost	13,000	10,400	9,900	8,250
Overheads:				
Set-up	5,200	6,500	3,900	3,900
Machine activity	8,974	9,573	8,974	7,479
Receiving	3,200	4,000	2,400	2,400
Packing & dispatch	5,200	4,160	3,120	2,600
Total cost	80,574	65,033	65,494	52,629
Unit cost	£8.09	£8.13	£10.92	£10.53

(c) Comparison

	A	B	C	D
Absorption basis—traditional	£8.35	£7.65	£11.09	£10.49
ABC	£8.09	£8.13	£10.92	£10.53

Absorption cost based on the following:

Percentage of direct labour cost of 196.2% (£81,500/41,550 × 100)

ABC overheads based on:

Set-ups	£19,500/15	£1,300 per set-up
Machine activity	£35,000/5,850	£5.983 per machine hour
Materials receiving	£12,000/15	£800 per production run
Packing and dispatch	£15,000/29,000	£0.52 per garment

Chapter 12

EXERCISE TABLE 12.1 Ambladec Ltd
Payback period is 2.67 years.
Net present value

Net Cash Inflows	Discount Factor 15%	Present Value £
Year 1 £100,000	0.8696	86,960
Year 2 £200,000	0.7561	151,220
Year 3 £300,000	0.6575	197,250
		435,430
Capital cost		400,000
Net present value		£35,430

EXERCISE TABLE 12.4   Ember Holdings

Machine retained for the full six years.

Net Cash Inflows	Discount Factor 12%	Present Value £
Year 1 £4,000	0.8929	3,571.60
Year 2 £6,500	0.7972	5,181.80
Year 3 £10,000	0.7118	7,118.00
Year 4 £9,000	0.6355	5,719.50
Year 5 £2,000	0.5674	1,134.80
Year 6 £1,500	0.5066	759.9
		23,485.60
Capital cost		24,000.00
Net present value		£(514.40)

This gives a negative NPV, suggesting the project is unviable.

Machine kept for four years only.

Net Cash Inflows	Discount Factor 12%	Present Value £
Year 1 £4,000	0.8929	3,571.60
Year 2 £6,500	0.7972	5,181.80
Year 3 £10,000	0.7118	7,118.00
Year 4 £9,000	0.6355	5,719.50
Year 4 £4,000 (scrap)	0.6355	2,542.00
		24,132.90
Capital cost		24,000.00
Net present value		£132.90

This at least produces a small positive NPV.

For the full six years:

> Initial capital cost = £16,800.00
> Capital cost at the end of year 3 = £18,000 × 0.7118 = £12,812.40
> Total capital cost = £29,612.40

Note. Where the capital cost is made later in the project, it too is discounted.

Total present values from (4) £23,485.60 less capital cost £29,612.40 give a negative NPV of £(6,126.80); unviable.

For three years:

First three years' inflows discounted = £15,871.40 less capital cost £16,800 also gives a negative NPV £(929), therefore also unviable.

INDEX